28

NorthStar

READING AND WRITING
Advanced

SECOND EDITION

Terra Brockman
Deborah B. Gordon

Series Editors
Frances Boyd
Carol Numrich

Writing Activity Book Editor
Helen S. Solórzano

Longman

NorthStar Writing Activity Book, Advanced, Second Edition

Pearson Education, 10 Bank Street, White Plains, NY 10606

Development director: Penny Laporte
Production manager: Debbie Sistino
Senior development editor: Paula H. Van Ells
Vice president, director of design and production: Rhea Banker
Executive managing editor: Linda Moser
Production coordinator: Melissa Leyva
Senior production editor: Kathleen Silloway
Director of manufacturing: Patrice Fraccio
Senior manufacturing buyer: Dave Dickey
Cover design: Rhea Banker
Cover art: Detail of Der Rhein bei Duisburg, 1937, 145(R 5) Rhine near
    Duisburg 19 x 27.5 cm; water-based on cardboard; The Metropolitan
    Museum of Art, N.Y. The Berggruen Klee Collection, 1984.
    (1984.315.56) Photograph © 1985 The Metropolitan Museum of Art.
    © 2003 Artists Rights Society (ARS), New York / VG Bild-Kunst, Bonn

Der Rhein bei Duisburg
Paul Klee

Text credits: **Page 6:** from "My Time in a Bottle," by Mickey Mantle. Reprinted
    courtesy of *Sports Illustrated,* April 18, 1994. Copyright © 1994 Time Inc.
    All rights reserved. **Page 24:** from "Gotta Dance," by Jackson Jodie Daviss.
    Reprinted with permission of the author from *Story,* Summer 1992.
    Page 71: from "We Are All Women Warriors," *Glamour.* Copyright © 1991.
    Page 72: from "In Peace, Warrior Women Rank Low," by James C. McKinley,
    May 4, 1996. Copyright © 1996. The New York Times Co. Reprinted by
    permission. **Page 79:** from *The Soloist,* by Mark Salzman. Copyright © 1994
    by Mark Salzman. Reprinted by permission of the author.
Text design: Quorum Creative Services
Text composition: Rainbow Graphics
Text font: 11/13 Sabon

ISBN 0-13-183299-9

Printed in the United States of America
1 2 3 4 5 6 7 8 9 10—VHG—09 08 07 06 05 04 03

Contents

Introduction

The *NorthStar Writing Activity Book*, Second Edition, is a companion to *NorthStar: Reading and Writing*, Second Edition. Building on the themes and content of the Student Book, the Writing Activity Book leads students through the writing process with engaging writing assignments. Skills and vocabulary from the Student Book are reviewed and expanded as students draft, revise, and edit their writing.

The Writing Activity Book was developed with the principle that the writing process and writing product are equally important. The units bring students step-by-step through the process of generating ideas, organizing and drafting content, revising their writing, and editing for grammar and mechanics. Students explore different prewriting techniques to find out what works best for them and for their topic. They experience the cyclical nature of writing, in which the writer is constantly evaluating and revising what is on the page. Through peer review exercises, students practice analyzing and responding to writing in a way that will help them better analyze their own writing. At the same time, they learn about the structural and rhetorical features of writing. They explore different ways to convey their ideas clearly depending on the purpose and audience of the writing assignment. They also learn how to use new grammatical structures in a meaningful context. Finally, they focus on editing and proofreading their writing for grammatical and mechanical correctness.

Design of the Units

The units are closely linked to the content of *NorthStar: Reading and Writing*, Second Edition. Therefore, it is essential that the books be used together. Each Writing Activity Book unit contains four sections that follow the writing process: Prewriting, Organizing, Revising, and Editing. The assignments are drawn from topics discussed in the Student Book readings and subsequent exercises. Teachers can choose to complete an entire unit in the Student Book before starting the writing unit. Alternatively, they can begin the Prewriting activities in the Writing Activity Book after completing the indicated sections in the Student Book and finish both units together. Checklists for the first, second, and final drafts remind students of which points to focus on in each draft.

1. Prewriting

Students complete Sections 1 to 3 in the Student Book before they begin this section. The activities in this section help students generate ideas and narrow a topic. They learn how to use a variety of prewriting techniques, such as freewriting, clustering, and brainstorming. Typically, students work together to analyze and manipulate a model prewriting exercise. Then they try using the prewriting technique on their own.

2. Organizing

In this section, students focus on organizing and developing their ideas. They learn about a structural or rhetorical feature of writing, such as writing topic and supporting sentences or organizing around a rhetorical feature, drawn from the Style section in the Student Book. They may analyze a model paragraph or organize ideas from the readings. Then they apply the ideas to their own writing. At the end of this section, students complete the first draft of the assignment and do a peer review exercise.

3. Revising

The activities in this section are designed to help students expand and polish their writing. The section has two parts. Part A, which is often drawn from the Style section in the Student Book, focuses on developing the content of students' writing. The activities help students achieve coherence and unity in their writing, clarify and improve the support for their ideas, or strengthen their introductions and conclusions. Part B, which is drawn from the Grammar section in the Student Book, helps students use the grammar point in a meaningful way in their writing. Students do exercises that use the grammar point in context. Then they look for places to apply the grammar in their writing. Although attention is given to grammatical correctness, meaningful usage is the focus. At the end of this section, students write the second draft of the assignment.

4. Editing

This section focuses on editing for grammar, form, and mechanics. Students focus on editing one feature in their writing. They identify and practice editing the feature in controlled exercises and then look for errors in their own writing. At the end of this section, students finish the final draft of the assignment.

Mickey's Team

OVERVIEW

Theme:	Addiction
Prewriting:	Freewriting
Organizing:	Creating a narrative
Revising:	Describing character Using past unreal conditionals
Editing:	Choosing word forms

Assignment

In Unit 1 of *NorthStar: Reading and Writing, Advanced,* Second Edition, you read about Mickey Mantle, who struggled throughout his adult life with addiction. Physical addictions are one type of personal struggle. Other challenges people face can be less threatening but no less important—for example, getting a new job or taking an important test. The assignment for this unit is to write an autobiographical or biographical essay. You will write about an addiction, personal struggle, or other challenge faced by you, a person you know, or a person you have heard of.

1 Prewriting

FREEWRITING

 Complete Unit 1, Sections 1–3, in the Student Book before you begin this section.

You are going to freewrite about an unhealthy addiction, personal struggle, or challenge you or someone else has faced. When you freewrite, you write as quickly as you can in order to record as many ideas as possible in a short amount of time. You should concern yourself only with ideas at this point. Do not worry about spelling or writing complete sentences.

Look at the example freewriting about nailbiting.

> Been biting my nails ~~for ages~~ ever since I can remember—was 5.
> Don't know why. Remember my grandmother offering reward to
> stop. How much? Think it was money, no—a pair of gloves. Didn't
> care about gloves at the time. Couldn't do it anyway. Never
> thought much about it, until I went to ~~college~~ high school. Someone
> during a test asked me to stop b/c the sound bugged her. Also I
> saw someone else doing it and it looked disgusting. In fact, I kept
> noticing other people doing it. But still couldn't stop. I'd try but
> then forget. Find myself doing it. Usually before I even knew I was.
> Often when reading or driving. Embarrassment/shame. I was always
> embarrassed about my hands. Often I bit the nails too far and
> they hurt.

1 *Before starting to freewrite, list some examples of unhealthy addictions, personal struggles, or challenges people face. Share your list with your classmates. Together, discuss the consequences of each addiction. For example, a consequence of TV addiction might be doing poorly in school or neglecting your family. How do the consequences make some of the addictions in your list seem more challenging than others?*

_____   _____

_____   _____

_____   _____

2 *Think about the person you want to write about. It can be you, a person you know, a famous person, or an imaginary person. On a separate piece of paper, freewrite for five to ten minutes about this person's problem. Use examples from this person's day-to-day life to explain the problem. You might want to write about how the addiction began and how it developed.*

3 *In small groups, share your freewriting. Ask questions or offer suggestions that might help the writer think of more details to include in his or her essay.*

2 Organizing

CREATING A NARRATIVE

Narratives tell a story. The events in a narrative are usually organized chronologically, in the order they happened. Narratives give the reader a clear, vibrant picture of the characters in the story and their feelings.

1 *Look back at Reading One in Section 2A in the Student Book. How is Mickey Mantle's autobiographical essay organized? Answer the following questions.*

- What is the chronology?
- How does the essay begin?
- What does the body of the essay describe?
- What does the conclusion summarize?

2 *Narratives, however, can also jump around in time. Read the beginning of an essay about a daughter's television addiction. Then answer the questions that follow.*

When she was 14 years old, the television became my daughter's best friend. After school, she would get her homework done as quickly as possible and then curl up on our old sofa in front of the TV, usually with a bag of something salty and a soda. In the beginning, I used to try to stop her from watching so much TV. I used to try to get her to do other things, but after a few months, I just gave up.

I believe my daughter's television addiction began as a way to escape from her loneliness and insecurities. The problem started when she was 13 years old and in junior high school. That year was a particularly painful one. First, I guess the problem began when we moved to a new town. She had a lot of problems making new friends. This might have been because she was still short for her age and perhaps not as thin as she could have been. But for whatever reason, a few weeks after school began, a few of the more popular kids decided it would be fun to be particularly mean to her. Within only a few weeks, she started growing terribly shy and insecure. I have always thought that if only she had been taller or thinner, perhaps things would have been different.

- What does the writer describe in the first paragraph?
- What does the writer describe in the second paragraph?
- How do you think the writer will continue the story?

3 *Time words and phrases show transitions between events or time spans in a narrative. Read the example paragraph again. Notice in the first sentence the phrase "When she was 14 years old" and in the second sentence the phrase "After school." These phrases help the reader follow the chronology of the narrative. Circle other time words and phrases in the paragraph. In pairs, compare your circled words. Discuss which words help the reader understand when the writer is jumping to a different time frame.*

4 *Look back at your freewriting. Think about how you want to organize your essay and what you want to say about the character(s). Make notes on the different aspects of the addiction or personal struggle. For example, you can focus on the following aspects:*

- the causes of the problem
- the manifestations of the problem
- the consequences and people affected by the problem
- how the person solved the problem

WRITING THE FIRST DRAFT

Use your freewriting and your notes to write the first draft of your essay. You may want to include the following in your first draft:

- **First paragraph:** This is a brief introduction to the person you are writing about and his or her problem.

- **Body:** The body contains two or more paragraphs on different aspects of this person's addiction.

- **Last paragraph:** Conclude your essay by summarizing the effect the personal struggle has had on you or the person who experienced it. You may want to discuss how things might have been different in other circumstances, what was learned from the experience, or how your or your main character's life has changed as a result.

Don't worry too much about grammar while you write; just concentrate on making your ideas clear.

PEER REVIEW

When you finish your first draft, exchange papers with a partner. Read your partner's first draft. While you are reading, do the following:

- Put a check beside the paragraph you like the best.
- Underline three sentences you think are particularly well written.

Reread your partner's paper, and do the following:

- Write three things you like about this essay.
- Put a check beside one paragraph that helps you to better understand the problem and the main character.
- Write any questions you have about any parts of the paper.

With your partner, discuss your reactions to each other's drafts. Make a note of any parts you need to revise.

3 Revising

A   DESCRIBING CHARACTER

Complete Unit 1, Section 4B, in the Student Book before you begin this section.

An autobiographical or biographical essay is effective when the reader is able to understand the personality and value system of the main character. The reader discovers qualities that may have influenced how the character faced a personal struggle or challenge.

1 *Read this excerpt from Reading One in the Student Book, and list the qualities of Mickey Mantle.*

> You are supposed to say why you ended up at the Center. I said I had a bad liver and I was depressed. Whenever I tried to talk about my family, I got all choked up. One of the things I really messed up, besides baseball, was being a father. I wasn't a good family man. I was always out, running around with my friends. My son Mickey Jr. could have been a wonderful athlete. If he had had my dad, he could have been a major league baseball player. My kids never blamed me for not being there. They don't have to. I blame myself.

2 *Work with a partner. Reread the example paragraph about a daughter's television addiction on page 4. List the qualities of the daughter. Then choose one of the qualities, and write two or three sentences of your own that show or describe that quality in this girl. Use your own ideas for these sentences. When you are finished, share your sentences with your partner.*

Example

> *She was so shy that she never wanted to talk to anyone. The few times she did get phone calls from girls in her class, she would ask me to tell them she wasn't home.*

3 *Look at your first draft. Is the main character well described? Are the character's values clear? Are all the issues and problems clear? Do all the parts of your essay help to clarify the issues and problems? If not, make notes on your first draft showing the changes you will make.*

B USING PAST UNREAL CONDITIONALS

Complete Unit 1, Section 4A, in the Student Book before you begin this section.

The past unreal conditional is used to express regret or to show how something could have been different under different circumstances. The past unreal conditional is useful when talking about negative situations such as addictions.

1 *Underline the **if** clauses in the conditional statements, and circle the result clauses. Then rewrite the sentences to explain what really happened.*

1. My son Mickey Jr. could have been a wonderful athlete. If he had had my dad, he could have been a major league baseball player.

   Reality: My son didn't have my dad, so _____

   _____

2. During my time at the Betty Ford Center, I had to write my father a letter and tell him how I felt about him. . . . I would have been better off if I could have told him that a long time ago.

   Reality: I wasn't better off because _____

   _____

2 *Think about something you (or the person you are writing about) regret. Write sentences using the past unreal conditional explaining what might have happened if you or your main character had done things differently. Share your sentences with the class.*

Example

> *I regret that I didn't spend more time with my son. If I had spent more time with him, we would have had a better relationship.*

3 *Look at your first draft. Did you use any past unreal conditionals? If so, are they correct? If not, find places to add one or two.*

WRITING THE SECOND DRAFT

Use the feedback you received from the peer review, your own notes, and comments from your teacher to help you revise your first draft. As you are writing, ask yourself these questions:

- Does the introduction clearly state the main character's problem?
- Can the reader understand the feelings, personality, and value system of the main character?
- Does each body paragraph talk only about one main idea?
- Are the body paragraphs in a logical order?
- Does the conclusion summarize the issues and problems?
- Is there at least one sentence using the past unreal conditional?

4 Editing

CHOOSING WORD FORMS

 Complete Unit 1, Sections 4A and 4B, in the Student Book before you begin this section.

1 *Read the paragraph. Decide whether the underlined words are in the correct form. Correct the word forms, if necessary.*

At first I thought the job was <u>manage</u>, although I could see it wasn't going to be easy. I was <u>determined</u> to do a great job and prove to everyone that I was <u>toughness</u> enough to handle it. However, in order to get everything done, I had to stay at work for extremely long hours. I was <u>surviving</u> on very little sleep and barely any food. I started to <u>avoidably</u> all my friends because I knew they'd just invite me out, and I didn't want to get distracted. I was overwhelmed and stressed most of the time. Nonetheless, I <u>priority</u> my work over everything else in my life. Soon I was spending all my waking hours at work. Then, a strange thing happened. I realized I really didn't want to be anywhere else. For a while, I <u>denial</u> it, but soon it became clear that I had become a workaholic. I couldn't stop and didn't want to stop.

2 *Look at your second draft for words that might be in the wrong form. Underline them, and check them in a dictionary. Where necessary, change the word form, or rewrite the sentence so that the word form is correct.*

PREPARING THE FINAL DRAFT

Carefully edit your second draft for grammatical and mechanical errors. Use the Final Draft Checklist to help you. Finally, neatly write or type your essay.

FINAL DRAFT CHECKLIST

- ❏ Is there an introduction that introduces the person and the problem?
- ❏ Is the chronological order of the events clear?
- ❏ Have you expressed the main character's feelings, thoughts, and values?
- ❏ Does the conclusion summarize the problems and issues?
- ❏ Are examples of the past unreal conditional formed correctly and used appropriately?
- ❏ Are word forms used correctly?

UNIT 2

A Season in Utopia

1 Prewriting

CRITICAL LISTING

 Complete Unit 2, Sections 1–3, in the Student Book before you begin this section.

1 *Review the Background reading in Section 1C, and Reading One in Section 2A in the Student Book. Use the information about utopias and Brook Farm to complete the critical lists below.*

Reasons People Create Utopias	**Reasons Utopias Fail**
create a more equal and fair society	*weak leadership*
have better work conditions	*financial troubles*

2 *Think about the assignment for this unit. Look back over your lists, and circle the three most compelling reasons to create or join a utopian community. Discuss with a partner why your circled items are important. Then look back over your list of reasons why utopias fail. With a partner, brainstorm ways in which the problems might be solved so that a utopia would not fail. Look at the following example.*

Problem	Possible solutions
Financial troubles	• *Make a financial plan or business plan to keep the community financially viable*
	• *Hire a financial analyst*
	• *Get a wealthy individual to finance the community*
	• *Make sure that there is good financial management, so that any problems are seen and addressed immediately*

3 *To gather and focus your thoughts, review all of your lists, placing stars by the ideas you think are most important. Use the starred items on your lists as the starting point for your freewriting.*

4 *Freewrite to discover more about your opinions regarding utopias—why they are formed and why they often fail.*

5 *Review your freewriting, and draw a conclusion about utopias. Is it possible for people to live in a community where there is peace, harmony, and justice for all?*

2 Organizing

REVIEWING THE BASIC FEATURES OF AN ESSAY

An essay consists of an introduction, a body of usually three to ten paragraphs, and a conclusion. The thesis (or main idea) is expressed in the thesis statement in the introduction. Each paragraph in the body provides information supporting the thesis. The conclusion restates the thesis, indicates how the main idea of each paragraph supports the thesis, and gives a suggestion or opinion.

1 *Read the following four paragraphs from an essay on visions of utopias and anti-utopias, or* **dystopias.** *The paragraphs are out of order. One of them is an introduction, one is a conclusion, and two are body paragraphs. Write* **I** *next to the introduction,* **C** *next to the conclusion, and* **B** *next to each of the two body paragraphs. Then order the body paragraphs* **1** *and* **2.**

_____ 1.   Even dystopias—dysfunctional, destructive, and doomed worlds—are important to imagine. In movies such as *Blade Runner, THX 1138*, and the *Terminator* films, our planet is destroyed physically. *Futurama, Earth: Final Conflict* and *Starship Troopers* all offer dystopian visions that grow out of a lack of morality, fascism, and extreme environmental crisis. These films are cautionary tales, examples of the horrible worlds that might become reality if we do not change our course.

_____ 2.   Ultimately, both dystopian visions and imagined utopias are important ways to analyze our present world and work toward a better future. It is the imagining of utopias, not the building of them, that is crucial. In our imaginations, walls drop from around the present and we gain the freedom to imagine a range of possible futures. For those whose imaginations have failed them, the future extends only to the next problem-filled day. But, for the rest of us, there remains a compelling need to imagine a better way to live.

_____ 3.   When Thomas More wrote his book *Utopia* in 1715, he gave a name to the vision of a perfect society. Today the adjective *utopian* has come into some disrepute and is frequently used to refer to something impractical or impossible. But the idea of utopia, a place where people will live in freedom, justice, peace, and harmony, is an important idea to hold on to. Visions of utopia reflect a conviction that in the future we will overcome inequities and injustices of the present. We live in a time when many people have lost this conviction and have become cynical and passive. We need to once again explore utopian ideas—through science fiction novels or dystopian films—as a first step toward creating a better future.

_____ 4.   Science fiction writing is one of the best forums for utopias, as it enables the author to create entirely new societies. Science fiction utopias grew out of late nineteenth-century socialist movements. H. G. Wells, Edward Bellamy, and hundreds of lesser-known authors created fictional visions of a better, socialist future. In his classic 1888 novel *Looking Backward,* Bellamy's hero wakes from a one-hundred-year sleep to the year 2000. In this imagined future, private property has been eliminated, and so humanity is free from scarcity, greed, and lust for power. Novelists like Bellamy, and later Ursula K. LeGuin and Kim Stanley Robinson, recruited millions worldwide to their anti-capitalist utopian visions.

2 *Look at the essay again. Answer the questions.*

1. What is the thesis?

2. Where in the introduction is the thesis stated?

3. How does each of the body paragraphs support the thesis?

4. Which sentence in the conclusion restates the thesis?

3 *Look back at your prewriting lists and freewriting on pages 11–12. Do you have more positive ideas or negative ideas about the possibility of utopia? What is your overall opinion about the success or failure of utopian communities? Write your thesis and main supporting points on a separate piece of paper.*

WRITING THE FIRST DRAFT

Use your prewriting lists, your freewriting, and the thesis and main points you listed to write the first draft of your essay.

- **First paragraph:** This is a brief introduction to the utopia or utopian idea you are writing about and your general opinion on it.

- **Body:** The body contains the ideas you wrote about in your critical lists and your freewriting. Allow these ideas to lead to more ideas and opinions.

- **Last paragraph:** Conclude your essay by summarizing the arguments that support your opinion. You may want to suggest a solution to some of the problems that utopias tried to address.

Don't worry too much about grammar while you write; just concentrate on making your ideas clear.

PEER REVIEW

When you finish your first draft, exchange papers with a partner. Read your partner's first draft. While you are reading, underline three ideas that you think are particularly interesting.

Reread your partner's paper, and do the following:

- Write three things you like about this essay.

- Make a note of the thesis of the essay (the author's opinion).

- Decide whether all the body paragraphs support that opinion.

- Write any questions you have about any parts of the paper.

With your partner, discuss your reactions to each other's drafts. Make a note of any parts you need to revise.

---

3 Revising

A   ANALYZING INTRODUCTIONS AND THESIS SENTENCES

 Complete Unit 2, Section 4B, in the Student Book before you begin this section.

1 *Which of the following statements describe the functions of an introduction? Which do not? Put an **X** beside the two that are not functions of an introduction.*

_____ 1. States the topic of the essay

_____ 2. Provides general background information

_____ 3. Provides a hook to make the reader want to read the essay

_____ 4. Presents a fact without expressing a point of view

_____ 5. Provides clear, detailed support of the thesis statement

_____ 6. States the specific focus and point of view of the writer

_____ 7. Indicates what the body of the essay will contain

2 *Read this introduction to an essay on the impossibility of a perfect society. Complete the tasks that follow. Discuss your answers with a partner.*

> (a) People have always sought an ideal society, a utopia. (b) Perhaps this is because of various myths about a "golden age" that existed long ago when everyone lived in peace and harmony. (c) Or perhaps it is simply part of human nature to want things to be better than they currently are. (d) But no matter how much we wish for a better society or a golden age, human nature prevents us from achieving it. (e) Visions of heavens soon turn into hells. (f) Because of the competitive and destructive aspects of human nature, utopias will always be an impossible dream.

1. Read the two ideas below. One is the topic of the essay, and one is the thesis statement. The topic of an essay is what the essay is about in general. The thesis statement states specifically the aspect of the topic discussed in the essay. The thesis statement often, but not always, appears at the end of the first paragraph. Label the topic **T** and the thesis statement **TS**.

   _____ Why utopias are sought but never become reality

   _____ Because of the competitive and destructive aspects of human nature, utopias will always be an impossible dream.

2. Read sentence (b). Why do you think the author introduces the idea of a mythical "golden age"?

3. Read sentences (a), (b), and (c). Do they relate more to the topic or to the thesis statement? Note that it is useful to explain and explore your topic sufficiently to persuade readers that the topic is interesting and important—worth their time and effort to read what you have to say.

4. Good introductions move gradually from general topic information to specific thesis statements. Which three sentences move the reader from the general information about the topic to the specific ideas of the thesis statement?

5. What do you think the next three paragraphs of this essay will be about?

3 *Look at your first draft. Is your introduction still appropriate? Is there a hook? Is there sufficient background information to explain your topic? Do the ideas develop from general to specific? Is there a thesis statement? Make notes on your first draft showing the changes you will make.*

B   USING NOUN CLAUSES

 Complete Unit 2, Section 4A, in the Student Book before you begin this section.

Incorrectly written noun clauses will make your ideas hard to read. Remember, noun clauses:

* can be subjects, objects of verbs or prepositons, or complements

* must have a subject and a verb

* are often introduced with question words, but the subject-verb word order is not inverted

1 *Identify and correct the noun clause errors in the following sentences.*

1. What have utopians never realized is that human nature will never allow a group to live peacefully and equitably.

2. Why choose to establish utopian communities is perfectly understandable.

3. It isn't always possible to know why the best solution to these problems is.

4. I'm not persuaded by your argument how does human nature prevent people from creating a better society.

5. Our society is unjust that was agreed upon by everyone.

2 *Look at your first draft for sentences that could be combined or improved with a noun clause. Add two or three noun clauses. Check that your noun clauses are correct.*

WRITING THE SECOND DRAFT

Use the feedback you received from the peer review, your own notes, and comments from your teacher to help you revise your first draft. As you are writing, ask yourself these questions:

- Is the opinion about the topic clear?

- Does the introduction contain a hook, background information, a gradual progression from general to specific information, and a thesis statement?

- Is the thesis statement well supported in each paragraph?

- Does the conclusion restate the thesis statement, indicate how the main ideas of the body support the thesis statement, and give a suggestion or state an opinion?

- Have I used noun clauses correctly and appropriately?

4 Editing

CORRECTING RUN-ON SENTENCES

Run-on sentences are two or more incorrectly joined independent or dependent clauses.

Example

Human nature always causes incurable problems visions of heaven turn into hell.

To correct a run-on sentence, do one of the following:

- Use a period to separate the independent clauses.

  Human nature always causes incurable problems. Visions of heaven turn into hell.

- Use a semicolon to separate the independent clauses.

  Human nature always causes incurable problems; visions of heaven turn into hell.

- Use a coordinating conjunction and a comma to join the independent clauses.

  Human nature always causes incurable problems, and visions of heaven turn into hell.

- Change one of the independent clauses to a dependent clause, and add a subordinating conjunction.

  Because human nature always causes incurable problems, visions of heaven turn into hell.

1 *Read and correct the following run-on sentences. Compare and discuss your answers with a partner. Note that there is more than one way to correct these sentences.*

1. One of the oldest utopian ideals is communism, *Plato's Republic* was communist, so was More's, as well that of Edward Bellamy, and of course the Soviet Union never fully achieved a communist society because it expected the impossible that people be less selfish than they are.

2. Utopians often exclude bad or weak types of people in *Plato's Republic* men and women were paired off to create smarter, stronger children the Nazis also wanted to purify and improve the race if that is utopia my vote would be to make do with the world we've got.

2 *Look at your second draft, and correct the run-on sentences.*

PREPARING THE FINAL DRAFT

Carefully edit your second draft for grammatical and mechanical errors. Use the Final Draft Checklist to help you. Finally, neatly write or type your essay.

FINAL DRAFT CHECKLIST

❏ Is the introduction clear and well supported by the body of the essay?

❏ Does the introduction contain a hook, background information, and a thesis statement?

❏ Is the essay divided into clear paragraphs with one main point for each paragraph?

❏ Does the conclusion restate the thesis statement and indicate how the main ideas of the paper support it?

❏ Are noun clauses used correctly and appropriately?

❏ Have all run-on sentences been corrected?

The Road to Success

OVERVIEW

Theme:	Personality
Prewriting:	Making a flowchart
Organizing:	Supporting main ideas
Revising:	Cohesion between paragraphs
	Using identifying and nonidentifying adjective clauses
Editing:	Subject-verb agreement

Assignment

In Unit 3 of *NorthStar: Reading and Writing, Advanced,* Second Edition, you read about people trying to achieve success. The meaning of success and the path to achieving it can vary from culture to culture and even from individual to individual. Think about your own personal definition of success, what would make you feel successful, and the qualities you need to reach your goal. The assignment for this unit is to write a descriptive essay about these qualities. You will describe these qualities and explain how they can help you achieve your personal dreams of success.

1 Prewriting

MAKING A FLOWCHART

Complete Unit 3, Sections 1–3, in the Student Book before you begin this section.

You are going to create a flowchart showing a path that leads to the attainment of a goal. Flowcharts are particularly useful for illustrating the steps toward a specific outcome. You begin by writing down your starting point, and then you write down all the possible steps to get to your goal.

1 Look at the following flowchart. The outcome is a career change. Work in pairs. Discuss the personal qualities required to ease the passage from one stage to the next. Write a quality for at least four of the different stages.

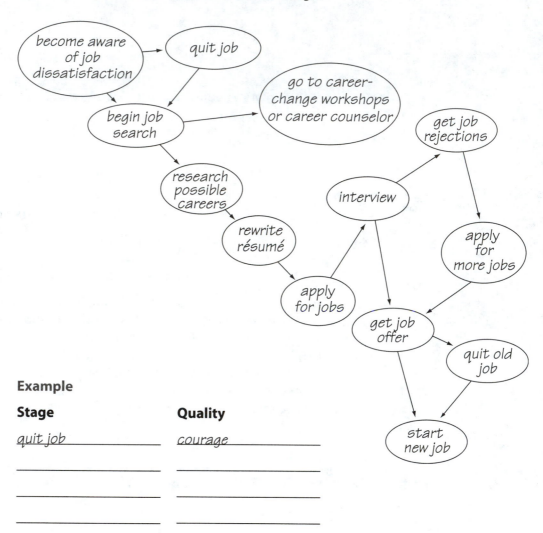

Example

Stage	Quality
quit job	courage

2 The strategies for building and maintaining self-confidence discussed in "Keeping Your Confidence Up," Reading Two in the Student Book, include learning from your failures, thriving on responsibility, making work fun, taking good advice, keeping your energy high, choosing commitment, accepting self-discipline, never accepting failure as a permanent state, and feeling gratified. With your partner, list three strategies that would be useful for the different stages of the process in the flowchart. Now think about the personal qualities, or traits, of Katie from "Gotta Dance," Reading One, and add any relevant ones to your list. Share your list with another pair of students or with the class.

3 *On your own, think of some personal goals or dreams. Choose one, and make a flowchart for it. Then assign personality traits or self-confidence-boosting strategies to various steps. Note that you do not have to attribute personality traits to each step. Circle the three personality traits or strategies that you think would best help you to achieve the success you want.*

4 *Freewrite about these traits and strategies. Why do you think they are important? How can they help you achieve your goal? Include notes on whether you feel you already have these traits or whether you feel you still need to develop them.*

2 Organizing

SUPPORTING MAIN IDEAS

 Complete Unit 3, Section 4B, in the Student Book before you begin this section.

Effective paragraphs are composed of two elements: a main idea expressed in a topic sentence, and ample support for the main idea. The purpose of support is to clarify the main idea because you, the writer, want your readers to understand exactly what you were thinking when you wrote those words. To do this effectively, you may need to provide more than one level of support—that is, you may need to explain your supporting details with additional details.

1 *Reread the paragraph below about entertainers (from Section 4B of the Student Book). What is the main idea of this paragraph? Which two well-known people does the author use as examples to support the main idea? Note how the author first introduces the examples and then explains how each example illustrates the main point.*

(a) Both Judy Garland and Marilyn Monroe were wonderful entertainers. (b) Although they died in the 1960s, they are still remembered today for their genius as performers. (c) Judy Garland was a fine actress and singer. (d) There isn't a child who doesn't know her as Dorothy in the classic film *The Wizard of Oz*. (e) Moreover, adults are still buying compact discs of her many record albums. (f) Marilyn Monroe played comic and tragic roles in films and on the live stage. (g) People today still watch videos of *Some Like It Hot*, *The Misfits*, and *Bus Stop*, her most famous films. (h) Yet both these actresses tried to commit suicide many times. (i) It is not clear if their actual deaths were the result of suicide attempts. (j) What is clear, however, is that despite their great successes, they were not happy people.

2 *Read the paragraph again. Write the letter of the sentence(s) in the paragraph that illustrates each description:*

_____ **1.** This sentence states the main idea of the paragraph. (Note that it is not the first sentence in the paragraph.)

_____ **2.** This sentence introduces the first example.

_____ **3.** These two sentences support the first example. They explain how the first example supports the main idea.

As you can see, the examples are the first level of support, and the remaining sentences are additional levels of support for each example.

3 *Read the following paragraph from Unit 3, Section 1C, of the Student Book. Then answer the questions*

(a) People's outlook on life has a lot to do with their potential for success. (b) Some researchers have found a direct link between hope and success. (c) They have found that optimists—people who always see the bright side of things—are more likely to succeed in life than pessimists, their direct opposites. (d) Hope does not just involve having a belief in good results. (e) It involves having both the will and the means to reach one's goal. (f) People with hope have some traits in common: They turn to friends for advice; they regard setbacks as challenges and not as failures; they know how to break a big goal into smaller chunks and work on one aspect at a time.

_____ **1.** Which is the topic sentence?

_____ **2.** What outlook on life is used as an example of the main idea?

_____ **3.** Which sentence introduces the example?

_____ **4.** Which sentence introduces the support for the example?

_____ **5.** How many sentences explain how the example supports the main idea?

Note that this paragraph does not have a concluding sentence that ties the supporting sentences together and relates them to the main idea. A concluding sentence is optional.

4 *Look back at the three personality traits or strategies you chose in Prewriting Exercise 2 on page 20. Choose one of those traits or strategies. Outline the levels of support you could use to explain why this trait or strategy is necessary for success.*

WRITING THE FIRST DRAFT

Use your flowchart, your list of personality traits, your freewriting, and your outline to write the first draft of your essay. You may want to include the following in your first draft:

- **First paragraph:** This introduction includes your definition of success, your personal goals, and a thesis statement defining the personal qualities you chose.

- **Body:** These three paragraphs define and illustrate three qualities with ample support. Remember to include supporting details that clarify your main ideas.

- **Last paragraph:** A concluding paragraph restates your thesis, ties your main ideas to the thesis statement, and/or makes a general statement about success and the path to achieving success.

Don't worry too much about grammar while you write; just concentrate on making your ideas clear.

PEER REVIEW

When you finish your first draft, exchange papers with a partner. Read your partner's first draft. While you are reading, do the following:

- Underline five sentences that you think are particularly well written.

- Check that each trait is clearly stated in a topic sentence.

Reread your partner's paper, and do the following:

- Make a note of the three traits the author chose.

- Note any places where you think more support is needed, and think about what the support might include.

- Point out any details that you think might not be relevant—details that don't help to clarify the main idea.

With your partner, discuss your reactions to each other's drafts. Make a note of any parts you need to revise.

3 Revising

A COHESION BETWEEN PARAGRAPHS

A cohesive essay is well organized and consists of paragraphs that have a clear relationship to each other. The ideas from one paragraph flow into the ideas in the next, and the reader easily understands the relationships between the paragraphs. Following are two techniques for creating cohesion between paragraphs:

- repeating key vocabulary

- repeating phrases to show how ideas are linked together

1 *How are the two techniques for creating cohesion used to link the second paragraph to the first? Underline the cohesive devices. The following is from "Gotta Dance," Reading One in the Student Book.*

At the bus station, I asked the guy for a ticket to the nearest city of some size. Most of them are far apart in the Midwest and I like the idea of those long rides with time to think. I like buses—the long-haul kind, anyway—because they're so public that they're private. I also like the pace, easing you out of one place before easing you into the next, no big jolts to your system.

My bus had very few people in it and the long ride was uneventful. . . .

Reread the last sentence. What if the sentence had been written in the following way?

There were very few people on my bus and the long ride was uneventful. . . .

Why does the original sentence provide more cohesion between the two paragraphs?

2 *Read three more pairs of paragraphs from "Gotta Dance": paragraphs 8 and 9, 13 and 14, and 19 and 20. With a partner, discuss how the techniques for creating cohesion are used to tie the pairs of paragraphs together.*

3 *Look at your first draft. Look for ways to make your essay more cohesive. Add at least two cohesive devices to your essay.*

4 *Work with a partner. Choose one of the paragraphs where you added a cohesive device. Read the paragraph and the one preceding it out loud to your partner. Read it first without the cohesive device, then with it. Ask your partner to identify the addition.*

B   USING IDENTIFYING AND NONIDENTIFYING ADJECTIVE CLAUSES

Complete Unit 3, Section 4A, in the Student Book before you begin this section.

Adjective clauses define, describe, or add information to the nouns or noun phrases in a sentence. Identifying adjective clauses are essential to identifying which person or thing you are referring to. Nonidentifying adjective clauses provide supporting information to further illustrate a noun or noun phrase, but they are not essential for identification.

1 *Complete the following sentences with the correct relative adverbs or pronouns from the box.*

who	which	whose	where
whom	that	when	

1. My ambitions, _____ were growing stronger every day, were guiding all my professional and personal decisions.

2. I took a course _____ promised to provide me with all the information I needed to get a job in my field.

3. The director of the program with _____ she interviewed was no longer an employee of the company.

4. Many people _____ want to succeed hold themselves back because of their fear of failure.

5. My friend, _____ own children had grown up, decided to become a foster parent, _____ fulfilled her need to help others.

2 *Look at your first draft. If you have not used any identifying or nonidentifying adjective clauses, find places to add them. Then check your adjective clauses:*

- Do they begin with the correct relative adverb or pronoun?

- Do they each have a subject and a verb?

- Are the nonidentifying adjective clauses separated from the significant clauses by commas?

WRITING THE SECOND DRAFT

Use the feedback you received from the peer review, your own notes, and comments from your teacher to help you revise your first draft. As you are writing, ask yourself the following questions:

- Does the introduction include a thesis statement that clearly states either that you are going to write about three personal qualities or specifically what personal qualities you are going to write about?

- Does each body paragraph talk about only one of your three personal qualities?

- Are there cohesive devices linking the paragraphs?

- Does your conclusion tie together your main points and your thesis statement?

- Have you used identifying and nonidentifying adjective clauses correctly?

4 Editing

SUBJECT-VERB AGREEMENT

1 *It is difficult to know whether to use a singular or plural verb with some subjects. The following chart outlines some of the problem areas in subject-verb agreement. Read the description of the subject. Read the example sentence. Then circle **S** (singular) or **P** (plural) for the correct verb form used.*

Subject Description	Example Sentence	Verb Form	
1. Singular nouns (including abstract nouns)	**Ambition is** essential for success.	S	P
2. Multiple singular nouns connected by the conjunction *and*	**Ambition *and* perseverance go** hand in hand for many people.	S	P
3. Singular noun followed by a prepositional phrase with a plural noun in it	Too much **self-confidence in young people** often **irritates** their coworkers.	S	P
4. Plural noun followed by a prepositional phrase with a singular noun in it	**Workshops on goal setting have** always been regarded as useful.	S	P
5. Expressions of quantity with plural nouns	**Most of the standards** of success **were** modified.	S	P
6. Expressions of quantity with singular nouns	At least **75 percent** of the money **has** been given to charity.	S	P
7. *Each, every,* and *everyone*	***Everyone* wants** to feel successful.	S	P
8. *Each of* + noun	***Each of* the candidates has** been interviewed individually.	S	P
9. Gerund as subject of the sentence	**Overcoming** my fear of speaking in front of many people **was** extremely difficult.	S	P

2 *Fill in the blanks with the correct form of the verb **be**.*

1. Maintaining high self-esteem _____ difficult in a profession in which you are in the public eye all the time.

2. Some of the goals I had set _____ too ambitious.

3. Most of the chapters of that book _____ on attaining financial success.

4. Success in those days _____ easier to attain.

3 *Look at your second draft. Check the subject of each verb, and decide whether it is singular or plural. Then check that the verb agrees.*

PREPARING THE FINAL DRAFT

Carefully edit your second draft for grammatical and mechanical errors. Use the Final Draft Checklist to help you. Finally, neatly write or type your essay.

> ### FINAL DRAFT CHECKLIST
>
> ❏ Is the essay divided into clear paragraphs with one main point for each paragraph?
>
> ❏ Are the main points written in topic sentences?
>
> ❏ Are all the main ideas well supported?
>
> ❏ Are identifying and nonidentifying adjective clauses used to define, describe, or add information?
>
> ❏ Are cohesive devices used to clarify the relationships between paragraphs?
>
> ❏ Do subjects and verbs agree?

Silent Spring

OVERVIEW	
Theme:	Social trends
Prewriting:	Making a flowchart
Organizing:	Focusing on cause or effect
Revising:	Writing unified essays
	Using discourse connectors to express cause and effect
Editing:	Identifying sentence structure

Assignment

In Unit 4 of *NorthStar: Reading and Writing, Advanced,* Second Edition, you read about how Rachel Carson started the modern environmental movement by writing *Silent Spring,* a book about the danger of pesticides. Since that time, many other environmental issues have gained the public's attention. Think of an environment-related issue that is important now but was not even an issue when you were younger. Why has it gained widespread attention? How has the attention changed the way people think and/or behave? The assignment for this unit is to write a cause-and-effect essay. You will write about a popular environmental issue.

1 Prewriting

MAKING A FLOWCHART

 Complete Unit 4, Sections 1–3, in the Student Book before you begin this section.

Effective cause-and-effect essays depend on clear relationships between causes and effects. Each effect may result in other effects, thus becoming a cause in its own right.

1 Look at the flowchart. Work with a partner. Notice the different paths in this flowchart. Notice also that there is some overlap between the ideas.

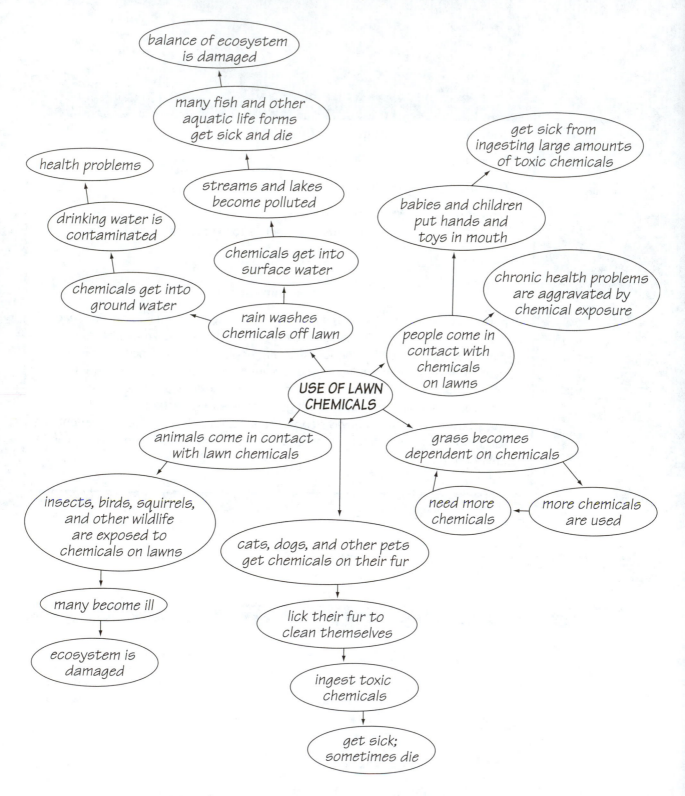

With your partner, do the following:

1. Write the words *cause* and/or *effect* next to each idea.

2. Circle the chain that you think sticks closest to the topic of lawn chemical over-use.

3. Decide which parts of the chain are not important.

2 *What specific environmental trend do you want to write about? First, freewrite on the topic. Then look at the ideas generated in your freewriting, and narrow your topic. Now make your flowchart.*

2 Organizing

FOCUSING ON CAUSE OR EFFECT

 Complete Unit 4, Section 4B, in the Student Book before you begin this section.

As you read in the Student Book, effective cause-and-effect essays usually focus on causes or effects, not both. Although it is almost always necessary to discuss both causes and effects, the discussion of one is usually the support for or the introduction to the other. Essays that focus on causes often explain why something is going to happen, might happen, or has already happened. Essays that focus on effects state possible or actual results.

1 *Look at the four common patterns of organization of cause-and-effect essays.*

- **immediate versus long term,** in which the immediate causes or effects versus the long-term causes or effects of a situation are discussed

- **coherent order of importance,** in which the causes or effects of a topic are discussed in a specific order such as chronological order or in order of importance from least important to most important or vice versa

- **order of familiarity or interest,** in which the causes or effects are presented in order of old information to new information

- **causal chain,** in which each effect is shown to be a cause for another effect

With a partner, look back at the flowchart on page 30.

1. Decide whether the focus of this flowchart is on causes or effects.

2. Decide which of the patterns described would best fit an essay developed from this flowchart.

3. Discuss how you would organize the ideas in the flowchart to fit this pattern.

2 *Skim "A Fable for Tomorrow," Reading One in the Student Book. Which of the four common patterns of organization do you think this essay most closely follows? Discuss your choice with a partner. Give reasons for your choice.*

3 *Think about how you would organize the ideas in your flowchart into a cause-and-effect essay. Choose one of the four patterns of organization. Think about how the ideas in your flowchart can fit into that pattern. Make some notes.*

WRITING THE FIRST DRAFT

Use your freewriting, your flowchart, and your notes to write the first draft of your essay. You may want to include the following in your first draft:

- **First paragraph:** An introduction includes background information on the topic, a brief explanation of how and why your environmental issue has gained popularity, and a thesis statement stating your focus.

- **Body:** These paragraphs focus on the cause or effect of the issue. Remember to support the main ideas with various levels of support.

- **Last paragraph:** A concluding paragraph restates the thesis statement, ties the main ideas to the thesis statement, and/or makes a general statement about what could or should be done about the issue.

Don't worry too much about grammar while you write; just concentrate on making your ideas clear.

PEER REVIEW

When you finish your first draft, exchange papers with a partner. Read your partner's first draft. While you are reading, do the following:

- Put a check beside the paragraph that you think is the clearest.

- Underline five sentences that you think are particularly well written.

- Decide whether the focus is cause or effect, and write *cause* or *effect* at the end of the paper.

Reread your partner's paper, and do the following:

- Make two lists, one headed "Causes" and one headed "Effects," and write all the causes and effects under the appropriate heading.

- Put a check beside clear and logical cause-and-effect relationships and a question mark beside any cause-and-effect relationships you have questions about.

- Make a note of which of the four organizational patterns the essay most closely follows. Tell the writer why and how you think the essay could be improved to more closely follow the pattern.

With your partner, discuss your reactions to each other's drafts. Make a note of any parts you need to revise.

---

3 Revising

A   WRITING UNIFIED ESSAYS

Unified paragraphs discuss only one main idea. That main idea can be supported in several different ways and at different levels, but all the supporting ideas must be directly tied to the main idea.

In the same way that unified paragraphs discuss only one main idea, unified essays make only one main point, expressed in a clear, focused thesis statement. Each paragraph serves as support to explain, illustrate, or show precisely what you mean in your thesis statement.

The challenge of writing unified cause-and-effect essays is to avoid letting causes lead to effects without relating them to your main idea. All paragraphs and all supporting statements within each paragraph must relate directly to the original cause or effect.

1 *Read the following thesis statement and outline of an essay on the increasing popularity of organic food. There are some unrelated details in the outline that, once the essay is written, would prevent the essay from being unified. Find the unrelated details, and cross them out. Then discuss your choices with a partner.*

Thesis statement

Organic foods have gained widespread popularity because they are raised in a way that is good for the plant or animal, good for the consumer, and good for the environment as a whole.

Outline

A. Introduction

B. Facts about organic food market

   1. Statistical information on the rapid growth of the organic market

   2. Large recalls of contaminated meat from non-organic sources

   3. Market research about consumers' food preferences

C. Facts about organic food production

   1. How organic fruits and vegetables are grown

   2. How organic meat animals are raised

   3. How air, soil, and water improve under organic farming methods

D. Facts about organic food consumption

   1. Most common reasons restaurant chefs and other food professionals prefer organic food

   2. Most common reasons consumers prefer organic food

   3. Most popular foods in the United States

E. How organic food has moved into the mainstream

   1. USDA standards for "Certified Organic" foods

   2. Consumer preference for tastier, healthier foods

   3. Good publicity on other food trends

F. Conclusion

2 *Look back at "The Story of* Silent Spring," *Reading Two in the Student Book. The author used the coherent order of importance pattern of organization. This pattern carries the reader along on an easy-to-follow chronological path that begins with Carson's first interest in the subject, her writing of* Silent Spring, *the book's publication, reactions to the book, and the book's enduring legacy. Even though the essay contains many details, the author has one point to make. Look back to the introduction to find that point. Write it in your own words.*

3 *Look at the conclusion of "The Story of* Silent Spring." *What sentence brings all the causes and/or effects in the essay back to the author's main point, showing that each paragraph supports this one point?*

4 *Look at your first draft. Write the main idea next to each paragraph, and then reread your thesis statement. Check that each paragraph has only one main idea and that this main idea relates to the main idea of the essay.*

B ## USING DISCOURSE CONNECTORS TO EXPRESS CAUSE AND EFFECT

 Complete Unit 4, Section 4A, in the Student Book before you begin this section.

Cause-and-effect essays use specific adverb clauses and/or discourse connectors to establish cohesion.

1 *On a separate piece of paper, make a table with two columns headed "Introduce a cause" and "Introduce an effect." Write the following adverb clauses and discourse connectors in the appropriate column:*

because	so	therefore	consequently	since	thus

2 *Read these additional common words and phrases used for establishing cause and effect in essays, and add them to the table you made.*

from	was caused by	as a consequence of	resulting in
due to	as a consequence	a direct result of	

*Now read the following sentences. Underline the discourse marker in each one, and decide whether it introduces a cause or an effect. Write **C** (cause) or **E** (effect) on the line. (Note that sometimes the addition of a preposition can change the relationship.)*

_____ 1. Many environmental issues gain popularity from the work of a small number of people.

_____ 2. As a direct result of the publication of *Silent Spring*, DDT came under strict government supervision and was eventually banned.

_____ 3. Carson's concern about DDT was caused by a letter from friends.

_____ 4. Carson carefully researched the facts in her book, resulting in 55 pages of notes and a list of experts who had read and approved the manuscript.

_____ 5. Due to intense lobbying by chemical manufacturers, many government regulations are weak.

_____ 6. During the past 20 years, food safety has declined; as a consequence, many people are growing their own food or getting it from local farmers' markets.

_____ 7. People were compelled to eat tasteless tomatoes due to their preference for uniform size, shape, and color.

3 *Look at your first draft. Underline the cause-and-effect markers you used, and check that you used them correctly. Look for other sentences that could be reworded by adding cause-and-effect markers to clarify the relationship between ideas.*

WRITING THE SECOND DRAFT

Use the feedback you received from the peer review, your own notes, and comments from your teacher to help you revise your first draft. As you are writing, ask yourself these questions:

- Does the introduction include a thesis statement that clearly states the focus on either causes or effects? Does it also include sufficient background information to interest the reader in the topic?

- Does each body paragraph focus on one main cause or effect? Is each paragraph well supported?

- Are there cohesive devices establishing the cause-and-effect relationships between the main points and the supporting details?

- Do all the paragraphs relate directly to the thesis statement or, in a causal chain organizational pattern, to the one before it?

- Does the conclusion restate the thesis statement and tie it together with the main points of each paragraph?

- Are discourse connectors accurately and effectively used to establish cause and effect?

4 Editing

IDENTIFYING SENTENCE STRUCTURE

Sentence structures vary from simple sentences consisting of one independent clause (**IC**) to complex sentences made up of independent and dependent clauses (**DCs**). To correct errors in sentence structure, you must be able to identify the different sentence types.

- Simple sentences (**S**) contain only one clause.

  The birds are silent.

- Compound sentences (**C**) contain two or more independent clauses joined by a coordinating conjunction such as *and* or *but*.

  |IC|IC|
  |The birds are silent,|and no one seems to care.|(Note that the clauses can also be joined by a semicolon.)

- Complex sentences (**CS**) contain two or more clauses, one of which is independent and at least one of which is dependent.

  |DC|IC|
  |Although the birds are silent,|no one seems to care.|

- Compound-complex sentences (**CC**) contain a combination of at least two independent clauses and at least one dependent clause.

  |DC|IC|IC|
  |Although the birds are silent,|no one seems to care,|but there is still time to| stop them all from dying.

1 *Label these sentences **S** (simple), **C** (compound), **CS** (complex), or **CC** (compound-complex).*

_____ 1. There was a strange stillness.

_____ 2. Then a strange blight crept over the area, and everything began to change.

_____ 3. The apple trees were coming into bloom, but no bees droned among the blossoms, so there was no pollination and there would be no fruit.

_____ 4. Developed in 1939, DDT was the most powerful pesticide the world had ever known.

_____ 5. Although Rachel Carson was a best-selling author, no magazine would agree to publish her idea.

2 *Look at your second draft. Try to identify the sentence type of at least five sentences. Then decide whether the structures are correct or should be changed.*

PREPARING THE FINAL DRAFT

Carefully edit your second draft for grammatical and mechanical errors. Use the Final Draft Checklist to help you. Finally, neatly write or type your essay.

FINAL DRAFT CHECKLIST

❏ Does the essay have an introduction, three or more body paragraphs, and a conclusion?

❏ Does the introduction have sufficient background information, a gradual shift from general to specific information, and a thesis statement indicating the focus on cause or effect?

❏ Does each paragraph include a topic sentence, sufficient support, and cohesive devices?

❏ Are each paragraph and the complete essay unified and coherent?

❏ Are all cause-and-effect relationships expressed effectively?

❏ Is the essay edited for sentence structure?

What Is Lost in Translation?

OVERVIEW	
Theme:	Cross-cultural insights
Prewriting:	Creating a Venn diagram
Organizing:	Analyzing methods of organization
Revising:	Writing thesis statements Comparing and contrasting ideas with adverb clauses
Editing:	Varying sentence types

Assignment

In Unit 5 of *NorthStar: Reading and Writing, Advanced,* Second Edition, you read about living in a multicultural society. Have you ever had a friend or known another family whose cultural values were different from yours? How did the differences affect your relationship? Did your similarities and differences contribute to your relationship? Did your relationship grow (or possibly dissolve) because of these similarities or differences? The assignment for this unit is to write a comparison-and-contrast essay. You will compare and contrast yourself, your family, or your culture with that of another person, family, or culture you are familiar with.

1 Prewriting

CREATING A VENN DIAGRAM

 Complete Unit 5, Sections 1–3, in the Student Book before you begin this section.

Good comparison-and-contrast essays compare and contrast things that have characteristics in common and characteristics that are different from each other. To clearly see the similarities and differences, it is useful to make a Venn diagram. Venn diagrams graphically represent the similarities and differences between two ideas or concepts.

1 *Read the lists of characteristics in this Venn diagram comparing Eva and Elizabeth from Reading One in the Student Book. Write **Eva** or **Elizabeth** in the appropriate side of the diagram.*

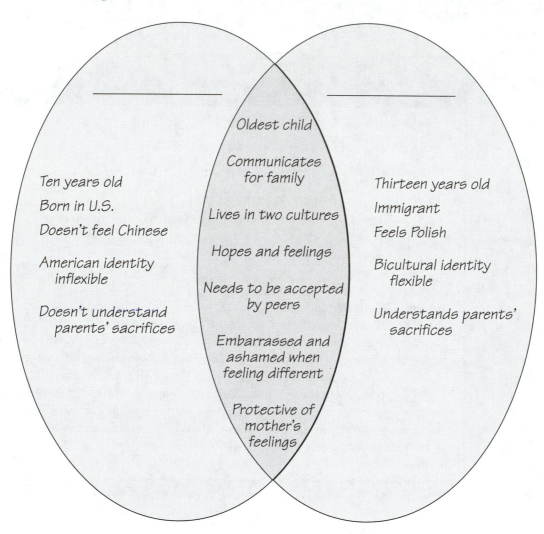

Ten years old
Born in U.S.
Doesn't feel Chinese

American identity inflexible

Doesn't understand parents' sacrifices

Oldest child

Communicates for family

Lives in two cultures

Hopes and feelings

Needs to be accepted by peers

Embarrassed and ashamed when feeling different

Protective of mother's feelings

Thirteen years old
Immigrant
Feels Polish

Bicultural identity flexible

Understands parents' sacrifices

2 *Put a check beside the most appropriate topic for an essay based on the Venn diagram.*

_____ **1.** Eva's situation is very different from that of Elizabeth because Eva is an immigrant and Elizabeth was born in the United States.

_____ **2.** Eva has a better relationship with her family because she is an immigrant.

_____ **3.** Elizabeth speaks better English than Eva because she was born in the United States.

3 *Before doing a Venn diagram, it is necessary to narrow the topic. Think about the assignment for this unit. First, with a partner, brainstorm ideas to narrow your topic.*

Examples

- cultural differences and how they affect friendships in the United States and another country I know well

- families and their methods of discipline

- importance of grandparents and children to family life in my Indonesian family compared to my friend's Egyptian family

4 *Choose a topic from your brainstorming ideas, and make a Venn diagram showing the similarities and differences of the various aspects of your topic.*

5 *Using your Venn diagram as a guide, freewrite about your topic to discover the aspects of your topic that you have the most ideas about or interest in.*

6 *Return to your Venn diagram, and add or change similarities or differences that arose from your freewriting.*

2 Organizing

ANALYZING METHODS OF ORGANIZATION

 Complete Unit 5, Section 4B, in the Student Book before you begin this section.

There are two organizational patterns for comparison-and-contrast essays: block organization and point-by-point organization. In a block organization essay, the similarities and differences between the two subjects are discussed in clearly distinct parts of the essay. In point-by-point organization, each paragraph discusses one "point," or category, that is common to both subjects.

   Although both organizational patterns can be used for any topic, some topics are more easily illustrated by one than the other. A point-by-point organization is often chosen when there are many complex aspects to a comparison; a block organization is more suitable for a simpler subject.

1 *In pairs, look again at the Venn diagram comparing Eva and Elizabeth in Prewriting Exercise 1. Discuss with your partner which of the two patterns of organization would be most appropriate for a topic based on this diagram. Discuss your reasons.*

2 *Using your chosen organizational pattern from Exercise 1, with your partner make an outline for an essay comparing and contrasting Eva and Elizabeth. Use the information from the Venn diagram and one of the two outlines in Section 4B of the Student Book as a guide. If you have any ideas of your own, add them and fill in supporting details where possible. Do not write which organizational pattern you are using on your outline.*

3 *Exchange outlines with another pair of students. Read their outline, and decide which organizational pattern they used. Discuss your decisions and the reasons for your choice of pattern.*

4 *On your own, decide which organizational pattern you would choose for the following topics. Write **B** (block) or **PBP** (point-by-point) on the lines. Then compare and discuss your answers with a partner.*

_____ 1. Compare and contrast appropriate job interview attire for Koreans and Nigerians.

_____ 2. Compare and contrast the development of the gender roles of recent male and female immigrants to the United States with that of the gender roles of nonimmigrant male and female U.S. citizens.

_____ 3. Compare and contrast the reading, writing, listening, and speaking second-language learning styles of Thai and Malaysian secondary students.

_____ 4. Compare and contrast the diet of the Alaskan Inuit people and the diet of the people of Greenland.

5 *Look back at your topic and your Venn diagram. Decide which organizational pattern is most appropriate for your topic. Then make an outline. Refer to the outlines in Section 4B of the Student Book to help you. Try your ideas in both types of outlines to see which one works better for your topic.*

WRITING THE FIRST DRAFT

Using your notes from your brainstorming discussion, your Venn diagram, your freewriting, and your outlines, write the first draft of your essay. You may want to include the following in your first draft:

- **First paragraph:** The introduction includes background information on your topic. Also include a thesis statement stating the purpose of your paper—what you are showing by comparing and contrasting this information.

- **Body:** Individual paragraphs compare and contrast the chosen aspects of your topic in either a block or a point-by-point organizational style.

- **Last paragraph:** A concluding paragraph restates your thesis, ties your main ideas to the thesis statement, and gives your reader something to think about regarding your topic.

Don't worry too much about grammar while you write; just concentrate on making your ideas clear.

PEER REVIEW

When you finish your first draft, exchange papers with a partner. Read your partner's first draft. While you are reading, do the following:

- Put a check beside the paragraph that you think is the clearest.

- Underline five sentences that you think are particularly well written.

- Decide whether the organizational style is block or point by point.

Reread your partner's paper, and do the following:

- Make a Venn diagram from the points compared.

- Determine if the support for the comparisons and contrasts is clear.

- Check whether there are any comparisons or contrasts that do not support the focus of the essay.

- Decide whether you think the author chose and followed the best organizational pattern for the topic.

With your partner, discuss your reactions to each other's drafts. Make a note of any parts you need to revise.

3 Revising

A   WRITING THESIS STATEMENTS

Thesis statements tell the reader what to expect. To do this clearly and effectively, thesis statements should not only state the topic or main idea of the essay, but also provide enough information for the reader to have expectations concerning:

- topics/main ideas of the supporting body paragraphs

- organizational pattern of the essay

Although you do not need to state every point you will make in the essay, it is important that your readers are able to form reasonably accurate expectations about the content.

1 *Read the following thesis statements, and predict the topics of the body paragraphs. Then compare your predictions with a partner's.*

    1. Due to both the subtle and obvious differences in North American and Asian business practices, it is recommended that people from both cultures receive cross-cultural training.

    2. Although the food sources for the Xantax and Qabal indigenous tribal people are very similar, their traditional diets are different enough to cause very different types of diseases in old age.

    3. To fully understand the differences between American and Samoan teenagers' relationships with their parents, you need to look at the differences in the parents' methods of discipline, expectations for help, and amount of time spent with their children.

2 *Because of their journalistic style, neither of the two readings in Section 2A, Reading One, has a thesis statement. On another piece of paper, write a thesis statement for each reading. Then compare them with a partner's statements.*

3 *Look at your first draft. Does your thesis statement state the main idea of your essay and provide the reader with enough information to form expectations concerning the main ideas of each paragraph? Rewrite your thesis statement so that it clearly states the main idea of your essay and how the main idea is going to be addressed.*

B   COMPARING AND CONTRASTING IDEAS WITH ADVERB CLAUSES

 Complete Unit 5, Section 4A, in the Student Book before you begin this section.

- Similarities and differences can be shown either within or between clauses. For example, you can say either of the following.

  Just as Eva is struggling to be accepted in Canada, Elizabeth is struggling to be accepted in the United States.

  Eva is similar to Elizabeth **in that** they are **both** struggling to be accepted in their respective countries.

- The following adverbials are commonly used to compare and contrast between clauses.

  Comparison or similarity: *just as, in the same way that, like*

  Contrast or difference: *whereas, while, despite the fact that, although, unlike*

- The following words and phrases are commonly used to compare and contrast within clauses.

  Comparison or similarity: *similar to, comparable to, both . . . and, as . . . as, like, is also*

  Contrast or difference: *more than, less than, different from, neither . . . nor, but, unlike*

1 *Reread "A Comparison of Eva and Elizabeth" in Section 4B of the Student Book. Underline the adverbials used to compare and contrast between clauses, and circle the words and phrases used to compare and contrast within clauses.*

2 *Look at your first draft. Did you use any of the adverbials listed to compare and contrast between clauses or within clauses? Rewrite your sentences so that both types of comparison and contrast are used. If you combined two clauses, check that you used commas correctly.*

WRITING THE SECOND DRAFT

Use the feedback you received from the peer review, your own notes, and comments from your teacher to help you revise your first draft. As you are writing, ask yourself these questions:

- Does the thesis statement provide enough information for readers to form expectations about the way the main idea is going to be addressed?

- If you used the point-by-point method, does each body paragraph focus on one point or aspect of your topic?

- If you used the block method, is the paper divided into distinct parallel parts? Is there a transition sentence that introduces the new parts?

- Are there enough examples or support to illustrate the points?

- Are there adverbials and other words and phrases that accurately illustrate comparison and contrast relationships between ideas?

4 Editing

VARYING SENTENCE TYPES

It is important to use a variety of sentence types in your writing, from simple sentences to complex sentences. (See page 37 in this book for a review of sentence types.)

1 *Read the following paragraph. What type of sentence is used most?*

> Although both my family and our next-door neighbors of 25 years are friends, we are very different. We celebrate different holidays. We eat different types of food. We even eat at different times of the day. We go to sleep and wake up at different times of the day and night. We speak different languages. We spend our money on different types of things. We even wear different types of clothes. Nonetheless, we have been very close friends for all the years we've been neighbors.

2 *With a partner, change the type of one of the sentences in the paragraph above to vary the sentence types.*

3 *Look at your second draft. Have you varied the sentence types? Often, just changing the sentence type of one of the sentences in the middle of a cluster of similar sentence types is enough to add variety. Look at the sentences in which you used adverbials to combine two clauses. Did you vary your sentence types by using the adverbial to start the second clause in some sentences and to start the first clause in others?*

PREPARING THE FINAL DRAFT

Carefully edit your second draft for grammatical and mechanical errors. Use the Final Draft Checklist to help you. Finally, neatly write or type your essay.

FINAL DRAFT CHECKLIST

- ❑ Does the essay have an introduction, three or more body paragraphs, and a conclusion?

- ❑ Does the introduction have sufficient background information, a gradual shift from general to specific information, and a thesis statement indicating the purpose for comparing and contrasting the subjects?

- ❑ Does each paragraph include a focused topic sentence and sufficient support?

- ❑ Is each paragraph unified and coherent?

- ❑ Does the essay follow either the block or point-by-point organizational pattern?

- ❑ Are the adverbials and other words and phrases used for comparing and contrasting used correctly?

- ❑ Is the essay edited for varied sentence type?

UNIT **6**

The Landscape of Faith

OVERVIEW	
Theme:	Religion
Prewriting:	Looped freewriting
Organizing:	Writing a definition essay
Revising:	Writing for a specific audience
	Using definite and indefinite articles
Editing:	Writing effective titles

Assignment

In Unit 6 of *NorthStar: Reading and Writing, Advanced,* Second Edition, you read a definition of the word *religion.* Were you brought up to follow a specific religion or philosophy of life? Is there a dominant religion in your home country? The assignment for this unit is to write a definition essay on the dominant religion in your country, or a religion or general philosophy of life you follow or are familiar with.

1 Prewriting

LOOPED FREEWRITING

 Complete Unit 6, Sections 1–3, in the Student Book before you begin this section.

Looping is a prewriting technique that is particularly useful either for generating ideas when you already know what your topic is or for narrowing down your topic.

To do looped freewriting, first freewrite on your topic. Then pick an interesting idea from your freewriting, and use this idea as the topic for a new freewriting. Repeat this procedure as many times as you need or want to.

1 *Think of the religion or philosophy you were brought up with as a child or are most interested in now. What are the defining beliefs in this religion or philosophy? What are its most important rituals, sacred objects, practices, and holidays? How does it manifest itself in the daily lives of those who follow it? How does it affect the goals and aspirations of its followers? What in particular do you find interesting about it? Freewrite about your topic, keeping these questions in mind.*

2 *Read your freewriting. Highlight the main ideas. Choose one highlighted idea, and use this idea as a topic for a new freewriting. Take a few minutes to discuss this topic with another student. Then freewrite about this new topic. Repeat the procedure as long as you find it useful. Alternatively, return to your original freewriting, and choose another of your highlighted ideas to freewrite about.*

2 Organizing

WRITING A DEFINITION ESSAY

 Complete Unit 6, Section 4B, in the Student Book before you begin this section.

A definition essay analyzes the different aspects of a topic. The analysis is achieved through classifying the subtopics of your topic into categories. A definition essay is similar to a one-sentence definition. A one-sentence definition relates the item being defined to a broader category of similar items and then shows how it is different from other members of its category.

Example

An <u>imam</u> is a <u>religious leader</u> in the <u>Islamic community</u>.

| **Member/** | **Larger** | **Specific** |
| **Smaller class** | **class** | **detail** |

A definition essay relates the essay topic to other similar topics (often in the introduction, or first paragraph of the body) and then defines the topic by illustrating the differences between it and the other members of its category.

Look at this outline of a definition essay.

A. Introduction: Classifies the topic (for example, a religious belief) into a larger category (for example, religion in general) and indicates a point of view

B. Body paragraphs: Define the topic by describing the important characteristics (for example, your religious beliefs and practices, leaders, or places of worship) and illustrating how they are part of a larger category

C. Conclusion: Restates the thesis statement and offers a personal perspective, a general statement, or a question on the topic

1 *Look again at your responses in Unit 6, Section 4B, of the Student Book. If these questions define a religion, then the answers to these questions constitute a definition of Buddhism. Using your responses, with a partner, expand on the outline of a definition essay. Include notes on the main ideas and supporting details you would write about in a definition essay on Buddhism. (Refer to Section 1C and Section 2A, Reading One, if necessary.)*

2 *Look back at your looped freewriting.*

1. What is the topic you are going to write about? What is the broader category it fits into? Make some notes on how your topic fits into this category—how it is similar to other members of the category.

2. What is your point of view on your topic? Make some notes. Then write a thesis statement including your point of view.

3. Underline the specific characteristics in your freewriting that differentiate your topic from the other members of the broad category in which it fits. Make an outline showing how you will discuss these specific characteristics.

4. Are there any terms in your freewriting that will need defining? List and then define them by stating their smaller class membership or item name, their larger class membership, and their specific details.

WRITING THE FIRST DRAFT

Use your looped freewriting, your notes, your outline, and your list of defined terms to write the first draft of your essay. You may want to include the following in your first draft:

- **First paragraph:** The introduction includes a thesis statement stating the topic you are going to define and your point of view.

- **Body:** These individual paragraphs define your various subtopics. Remember to include similarities with and differences from similar concepts, examples, and any other details that will effectively communicate and support your main ideas.

- **Last paragraph:** A conclusion restates the thesis and shows how the main ideas in the body support your initial definition and your point of view.

Don't worry too much about grammar while you write; just concentrate on making your ideas clear.

PEER REVIEW

When you finish your first draft, exchange papers with a partner. Read your partner's first draft. While you are reading, do the following:

- Put a check beside the paragraph that you think best defines the topic.

- Underline five sentences that you think are particularly well written.

Reread your partner's paper, and do the following:

- Make a note of the broad category the author uses to define the topic.

- Make a note of the specific details the author uses to define the topic.

- Note whether the author expresses a point of view concerning the topic.

- Note whether each paragraph discusses related specific details and includes sufficient examples and support.

- Write any questions you may have about any of the author's points.

With your partner, discuss your reactions to each other's drafts. Make a note of any parts you need to revise.

3 Revising

A   WRITING FOR A SPECIFIC AUDIENCE

Regardless of the type of writing you are doing, it is always important to write for a specific audience, or reader, and with a specific purpose or reason in mind. Writing for a specific audience is particularly important for definition essays, as you need to know what your reader knows and understands about your topic before you can decide how to define your topic. Your intended audience should drive your choice of content; the way you choose to present your topic; the amount of detail you use to explain and support each point; your style, tone, and level of formality; and even the words and grammatical structures you choose to use.

1 *Work in pairs. Read the following writing types, any of which could include definition essays, and match them with appropriate purposes. Note there may be more than one answer. Discuss the reasons for your choices.*

Writing Types

_____ 1. newspaper editorial

_____ 2. newspaper or magazine article exposing a problem

_____ 3. textbook

_____ 4. short story

_____ 5. product analysis

_____ 6. research paper

_____ 7. report

_____ 8. technical manual

Purposes

a. present author's knowledge

b. entertain

c. inform

d. persuade

e. explain how to accomplish a task

f. sell

g. advise

h. initiate change

2 *With your partner, decide on a possible audience for the writing types listed.*

Example

The reader of a consumer report would probably be a buyer or consumer.

3 *Imagine that your purpose for this paper is to inform an academic audience that is completely unfamiliar with the religion or philosophy of life you are defining. Imagine that your audience has never had a close friend of that religion, never visited a country where the religion is widely practiced, comes from a completely different background, and follows a completely different religion or philosophy of life. Try to imagine that you are your uninformed reader. Look at your first draft from your reader's perspective:*

- Look for places where you might have made assumptions about your reader's knowledge of the topic.

- Are all the terms defined that need defining?

- Are enough supporting details included to communicate the ideas clearly to the uninformed reader?

- Make notes of the additional information you will need to add to your first draft to make the ideas clear to your audience.

B   USING DEFINITE AND INDEFINITE ARTICLES

Complete Unit 6, Section 4A, in the Student Book before you begin this section.

1 *Read the following nouns, many of which come from the readings in Unit 6 of the Student Book. Write **C** (count) or **NC** (non-count) next to each one. Some words can be count or non-count words, depending on the context. If you are unsure of any of the meanings, look up the words in a dictionary.*

_____ honesty	_____ law	_____ belief
_____ principle	_____ knowledge	_____ ritual
_____ evil	_____ generosity	_____ forgiveness
_____ reincarnation	_____ prayer	_____ hypocrisy
_____ symbol	_____ faith	_____ kindness
_____ goodness	_____ commitment	_____ creation
_____ guideline	_____ tenet	_____ acceptance
_____ (in)tolerance	_____ charity	_____ tradition
_____ death		

2 *Check your answers with a partner. Then, in pairs, choose two non-count nouns and two count nouns, and write one sentence for each one. Take care that your use of indefinite or definite articles is correct.*

3 *Reread the list of words. Find at least four words from the list that apply to your topic. Then look at your first draft, and find places to include these concepts in your definitions and/or discussion. Keep in mind that you may need to add supporting sentences or possibly new paragraphs.*

4 *Check the other nouns in your paper, and decide if they are count or non-count nouns. Then check your use of definite and indefinite articles.*

WRITING THE SECOND DRAFT

Use the feedback you received from the peer review, your own notes, and comments from your teacher to help you revise your first draft. As you are writing, ask yourself these questions:

- Does the introduction clearly state what is going to be defined, and the point of view?

- Does the essay define and explain the topic well enough for a reader who is completely unfamiliar with it?

- Are enough examples used? Do similarities with and differences from other philosophies help to effectively define the topic?

- Does the conclusion restate the thesis statement and tie together focus, point of view, and all the main points? Does it leave the reader with something to think about?

- Is the use of definite and indefinite articles with count and non-count nouns correct?

4 Editing

WRITING EFFECTIVE TITLES

The title of your essay may be the first thing the reader notices. The title has two main functions:

- to spark enough interest in the reader to want to read your essay

- to provide sufficient information to allow the reader to make predictions about the content of your essay

1 *Read the following list of essay titles.*

Religious Conflicts through the Centuries

Living in Harmony with Your Inner Self

A Day in the Life of a Teenage Tibetan Monk

Religious Conversion: Can It Work for You?

Why I Rejected My Parents' Religion

Intermarriage—Answering Your Children's Questions

A Philosophy, a Religion, and a Code to Live By

Blind Faith

Devotion

Living by the Golden Rule

Do You Really Live Your Religion?

Read the seven essay title guidelines. Circle the correct word in parentheses.

Essay Title Guidelines

1. Essay titles should be brief, not more than (five / ten / twenty) words.

2. Titles can be as short as (three words / one word / two words).

3. Titles (are / aren't) usually sentences.

4. Titles (can / can't) be questions.

5. Titles (can / can't) include punctuation such as question marks, hyphens, commas, colons, or semicolons but (can / cannot) have periods at the end.

6. Usually, prepositions of fewer than (three / four / five) letters are not capitalized.

7. The first and last words of a title are capitalized (even if / unless) they are articles or short prepositions.

---

2 *With a partner, choose the three titles in the list that you find the most interesting. Make some predictions about what you think the main points of these essays would be.*

3 *Exchange your second draft with your partner. Read your partner's paper and title. Make recommendations as to how your partner can improve the title.*

PREPARING THE FINAL DRAFT

Carefully edit your second draft for grammatical and mechanical errors. Use the Final Draft Checklist to help you. Finally, neatly write or type your essay.

FINAL DRAFT CHECKLIST

❏ Does the essay have an effective introduction, three or more body paragraphs, and a conclusion?

❏ Does each paragraph include a focused topic sentence and sufficient support with examples and comparisons to further clarify the explanations and definitions for a reader unfamiliar with the topic?

❏ Is the essay unified and coherent?

❏ Is the essay targeted to a specific audience?

❏ Is the essay edited for the use of definite and indefinite articles with count and non-count nouns?

❏ Does the essay title interest the reader and provide enough information for essay content prediction?

Going into Business

Theme:	Business
Prewriting:	Clustering
Organizing:	Weighing pros and cons
Revising:	Writing effective conclusions
	Using infinitives and gerunds
Editing:	Using transition words

Assignment

In Unit 7 of *NorthStar: Reading and Writing, Advanced,* Second Edition, you read about young entrepreneurs who started their own businesses and about the hiring practices of a large corporation. If you had the opportunity to either start your own business or be part of a large company such as Coca-Cola, how would you analyze the options and make a choice? The assignment for this unit is to write an essay that analyzes the advantages and disadvantages of working for an existing company versus starting a business of your own. After you weigh the pros and cons, conclude the essay by stating why you would or would not want to work for a large company.

1 Prewriting

CLUSTERING

 Complete Unit 7, Sections 1–3, in the Student Book before you begin this section.

Clustering is useful for generating and linking ideas about a topic. A cluster diagram helps you visualize the relationships between your ideas.

Most cluster diagrams begin with the topic of the essay in a circle in the center. Related ideas or subtopics are then circled and linked to the other ideas by lines.

1 *Look at the cluster diagram. What is the topic of the essay?*

2 Some of the ideas in the cluster diagram are positive, and some are negative. Label them **P** (positive) or **N** (negative).

3 Work with a partner. Discuss whether the author of this cluster diagram feels that owning his or her business would be more of a positive or a negative experience. What might the author's thesis statement be? Discuss whether the author's essay would be stronger if it included both positive and negative aspects of the topic.

4 Look at the assignment for the unit. Make a cluster diagram for the topic of working for a large successful company such as Coca-Cola. Write your topic in the center of a clean piece of paper, and then add as many subtopics and related ideas as you can.

5 Look at your cluster diagram, and analyze the subtopics. Are there any subtopics that you can add ideas to, combine, separate, or delete altogether? Label ideas in the cluster diagram as **P** (positive) or **N** (negative). Do you think there are more advantages or disadvantages associated with working for a large company? Write a preliminary thesis statement.

6 Freewrite about your topic using your thesis statement and ideas from your cluster diagram. Remember that clustering helps you discover your own ideas. It is possible that on reflection you will decide that some ideas in your cluster are not suitable for your essay.

2 Organizing

WEIGHING PROS AND CONS

 Complete Unit 7, Section 4B, in the Student Book before you begin this section.

An analysis essay weighing pros and cons is often organized in a point-by-point or block pattern, similar to the organization of a comparison-and-contrast essay (see Unit 5). In the block organization, advantages will be discussed in one section of the essay and disadvantages in another. In the point-by-point organization, each paragraph discusses one point, including pros and cons relating to that point. You may spend more time on advantages or disadvantages, but a good analysis essay addresses both.

Not all analysis essays draw conclusions, but in your analysis essay you will conclude by stating whether you think advantages outweigh disadvantages or vice versa. To come to a strong conclusion, you may use an additional organizational pattern, sequencing your ideas by order of importance. The most important point is stated either first or last.

1 *Work with a partner. Look at Readings One and Two in Unit 7 of the Student Book, and answer the following questions.*

Reading One

1. Who is the audience for this article: people who may start their own businesses, or people who will probably work for an existing company?

2. What is the writer's purpose in this article?

3. The article mentions a number of advantages of entrepreneurship: the opportunity to make a lot of money, to create your own work environment, to have creative control, and to do something that is important to you. However, one of the people does not really want to be an entrepreneur. Which person is it? What disadvantages are mentioned?

4. Is this article focused more on the advantages or disadvantages of entrepreneurship?

5. If the writer had drawn a conclusion at the end of this article, what do you think it would have been?

6. If you were to use information from this reading in the body of your analysis essay, would it support the advantages or disadvantages of entrepreneurship?

Reading Two

1. Where is this article from?

2. Who is the audience for this article?

3. What is the main idea of the article?

4. How many approaches to recruiting and keeping employees does the article mention? Is any one approach more important than another? Are any disadvantages to this recruiting emphasis mentioned?

5. If you were to use information from this reading in your analysis essay, would it be to discuss the advantages or disadvantages of working for a large multinational company?

2 *Look back at your cluster diagram and your freewriting. Do you think there are more advantages or disadvantages to working for an existing company rather than starting your own company? Make notes on your ideas, and then organize your ideas in a block or point-by-point outline. You may follow the guidelines for point-by-point outlining on page 120 of Unit 5 of the Student Book.*

WRITING THE FIRST DRAFT

Use your cluster diagram, freewriting, and outline to write the first draft of your essay. You may want to include the following in your first draft:

- **First paragraph:** State your purpose in writing the essay, and take a stand on the issue. In your thesis statement, tell why you think there are more advantages or disadvantages to working for an existing company rather than starting your own business.

- **Body:** Build support for your thesis by discussing advantages and disadvantages. If you think disadvantages outweigh advantages, then more of the body will be concerned with the disadvantages, or vice versa. Remember to use transition words and include reasons, examples, facts, and other supporting details that will build support for your conclusion.

- **Last paragraph:** State the conclusion you have been building toward, and summarize your support for this conclusion.

Don't worry too much about grammar while you write; just concentrate on making your ideas clear.

PEER REVIEW

When you finish your first draft, exchange papers with a partner. Read your partner's first draft. While you are reading, do the following:

- Put a check beside the advantage or disadvantage that you think is best explained.

- Underline five sentences that you think are particularly well written.

Reread your partner's paper, and do the following:

- Make a note of whether the author organized the essay in blocks or point by point.

- If the author used blocks, was the block of advantages or disadvantages more convincing?

- If point-by-point order was used, did the author provide a compelling analysis of each point, weighing the pros and cons?

- Are there any ideas that you don't understand or that you would like more information about?

With your partner, discuss your reactions to each other's drafts. Make a note of any parts you need to revise.

3 Revising

A WRITING EFFECTIVE CONCLUSIONS

The purpose of a conclusion is to bring your essay to a close. A strong, effective conclusion will keep your ideas in the reader's mind and may even change his or her mind about the topic. Effective conclusions can do the following:

- summarize the main points of the essay and restate the thesis
- re-emphasize the writer's position on the topic
- restate the thesis in a new way, adding a new twist or way of thinking about the topic based on the points you raised in the body
- summarize the main ideas in the body of the essay and/or show how the main ideas support the thesis statement and lead inevitably to the conclusion
- re-emphasize the importance of the topic so that the reader feels he or she has learned something

1 *The main idea of "Coca-Cola Thinks International," Reading Two in the Student Book, is that the Coca-Cola company has been successful internationally in part because of its recruitment policies. Reread the conclusion. Which sentence restates that main idea?*

2 *The first paragraph in the body of "Coca-Cola Thinks International" describes Coca-Cola's multilingual, multicultural emphasis. The second paragraph describes its recruitment of college students. Which sentence in the conclusion draws these two paragraphs together and ties them to the main idea?*

3 *Reread the conclusion to "The Advantages and Disadvantages of Private Business Schools" (pages 166–167 of the Student Book). Now reread the introduction, and skim the body of the essay. With your partner, discuss the purpose of this conclusion. Which of the purposes above does this conclusion mainly fill?*

4 *Reread Reading One, "Who Wants to Be an Entrepreneur?" Write a conclusion to this reading that fulfills the following criteria:*

- It re-emphasizes the importance of the topic so that the reader feels he or she has learned something.
- It re-emphasizes the writer's position on the topic.

5 *Exchange your first draft with a partner. Read the introduction and the body of the paper, but do not read the conclusion. Write a conclusion for your partner's paper. Discuss each other's new conclusions, and compare them with the originals.*

6 *Look at your first draft. Rewrite your conclusion using the best parts of your original conclusion and the conclusion your partner wrote.*

B USING INFINITIVES AND GERUNDS

Complete Unit 7, Section 4A, in the Student Book before you begin this section.

1 *Some of following sentences are incorrect. Put a check beside the sentences that are incorrect. Cross out the errors, and write the correct forms.*

_____ **1.** Although I have no professional experience working for a computer company, I've always found it easy to work with computers.

_____ **2.** I think I have a natural ability run a business.

_____ **3.** I would love to have the opportunity to use my creativity to start an advertising business.

_____ **4.** I do not think I would have any difficulty in getting clients to trusting me and even to relying on me.

_____ **5.** After work for some years, I would be very interested in have the responsibility for expanding my business.

_____ **6.** I'm sure that after some years in one business, I would be ready to move into a CEO position at another business.

2 *Choose three infinitive and three gerund phrases in Unit 7, Section 4A, of the Student Book, and use them to write sentences about your topic.*

3 *Look at your first draft, and check your use of infinitives and gerunds.*

WRITING THE SECOND DRAFT

Use the feedback you received from the peer review, your own notes, and comments from your teacher to help you revise your first draft. As you are writing, ask yourself these questions:

- Does the introduction clearly state the thesis?

- Does the essay analyze advantages and disadvantages and explain the writer's overall views?

- Is the essay sequenced in blocks or point by point? Is the most important idea presented first or last?

- Does the conclusion restate the thesis and tie together all the main points? Does it also suggest other ideas for the reader to think about or re-emphasize the writer's position on the topic?

- Are gerund and infinitive phrases used correctly?

4 Editing

USING TRANSITION WORDS

Many transition words are used when analyzing advantages and disadvantages. Some transition words help you introduce supporting details such as reasons, examples, and facts. Other transition words can help express the order of importance of your ideas.

1 *Read the sentences below. They contain underlined transition words and phrases. Write* **SD** *if it introduces supporting details or* **OI** *if it expresses order of importance.*

<u>SD</u> **1.** Getting a part-time job while you are still in high school has both advantages and disadvantages. <u>On the plus side</u>, a part-time job is a good way to make a little extra money.

_____ **2.** <u>Also</u>, a part-time job gives you work experience that will help you get a better job when you are done with school.

_____ **3.** <u>For example</u>, my friend Bill had a part-time job at a gas station, and now he is a full-time mechanic.

_____ **4.** Part-time jobs can help you earn money and get experience, <u>but above all</u> they give you a chance to see what work in the "real world" is all about.

_____ **5.** However, for every plus there is a minus. <u>For one thing</u>, spending time at a job means you will spend less time studying or sleeping.

_____ **6.** It is <u>particularly</u> difficult to do well at school when you are tired and have not studied. Some students even drop out of school.

_____ **7.** <u>More significant</u> than the time a job takes away from sleeping and studying are the benefits of part-time jobs, which help students get ready for the "real world" of employment by giving them money, experience, and a sense of adult responsibilities.

2 *Read the sentences again. Discuss with a partner which of the following transition words could be used to replace the underlined words in each sentence to keep the same meaning.*

one disadvantage is that	one advantage is that	in addition
more important	for instance	most important
especially		

3 *Look at your second draft. Have you used appropriate transition words to introduce supporting details or order of importance? If not, find places to add them.*

PREPARING THE FINAL DRAFT

Carefully edit your second draft for grammatical and mechanical errors. Use the Final Draft Checklist to help you. Finally, neatly write or type your essay.

FINAL DRAFT CHECKLIST

- ❏ Does the essay have an effective introduction, three or more body paragraphs, and a strong conclusion?
- ❏ Does each paragraph include a focused topic sentence and sufficient support with examples?
- ❏ Are the paragraphs organized either in block order or point by point?
- ❏ Does the conclusion restate the thesis and fulfill one of the criteria discussed in Section 3A on page 62?
- ❏ Are transition words used to introduce supporting details or order of importance?
- ❏ Is there an interesting title?

UNIT 8

When the Soldier Is a Woman . . .

OVERVIEW

Theme:	The military
Prewriting:	Focused freewriting*
Organizing:	Using persuasive reasons to support your point of view
Revising:	Supporting your reasons with examples Incorporating direct and indirect speech
Editing:	Punctuating direct quotes

Assignment

In Unit 8 of *NorthStar: Reading and Writing, Advanced,* Second Edition, you read that allowing women into the military is fraught with controversy. There are advantages and disadvantages for the country, for women, and for men. What role do you think women should have in your country's military? The assignment for this unit is to write a persuasive essay explaining your opinion.

1 Prewriting

FOCUSED FREEWRITING

 Complete Unit 8, Sections 1–3, in the Student Book before you begin this section.

---

* Focused freewriting is an adaptation of a prewriting strategy called "cubing," from Rebecca Mlynarczyk and Steven B. Haber, *In Our Own Words,* (New York: St. Martin's Press, 1996), pp. 215–216.

Focused freewriting is useful for both generating ideas and narrowing your topic. When you use focused freewriting, you freewrite on five distinct categories, or aspects, of the topic:

1. **definition/description:** definitions, facts, examples, and/or general or physical characteristics

2. **personal application:** your own personal experiences. Do you know someone who has been affected by your topic, or have you personally been affected by it in some way? Do you have any memories or personal stories to share?

3. **comparison/contrast:** discussion of similarities and differences between your topic and a comparable topic

4. **critical evaluation:** your reasons or feelings, other people's opinions or feelings, any controversies and/or evidence

5. **practical uses:** changes your topic might bring about. How can your topic affect society or the government? Can your topic solve any problems? What recommendations would you make regarding this topic?

1 *Work with a partner, and brainstorm ideas about women and the military. Brainstorm ideas in each of the five topic categories.*

2 *Choose a category. Think about the unit assignment, and freewrite on this aspect of your topic. Then choose another category, and freewrite on your topic from this new perspective. Repeat the procedure with each of the remaining three categories.*

3 *Reread each of your focused freewritings, and underline the important and useful ideas in each one. Look for the supporting reasons you will use to defend your point of view. Note that focused freewriting does not produce a first draft. It simply generates ideas, some that will be useful in your first draft and some that may not be so useful.*

2 Organizing

USING PERSUASIVE REASONS TO SUPPORT YOUR POINT OF VIEW

Persuasive essays are written for two purposes:

- to clearly express your opinion about a topic

- to convince someone to change his or her mind about something

Many writers are successful only in clearly expressing their opinion. They fail to change their readers' minds because they use their own opinions, unsupported generalizations, and faulty logic to support their thesis. To convince your reader that your thesis is valid, you need to support your thesis with reasons based on established facts rather than opinions and unsupported generalizations. In addition, the established facts you use to prove your opinions might also need to be supported with more facts.

Unpersuasive Support

Opinion: A volunteer army is the solution to the current high rate of unemployment.
Unsupported generalization: All army officials prefer a volunteer army.
Faulty logic: The volunteer military is not having any trouble filling its ranks at present as a result of the high degree of global political turmoil.

Persuasive Support

Supported fact: A volunteer military is not filled with people who have low educational goals. One 2003 report noted that the majority of new recruits joined the military with the intention of enrolling in college classes while enlisted in the military.

1 *Read the following list of facts, opinions, unsupported generalizations, and examples of faulty logic. Identify the facts (**F**) and opinions (**O**).*

_____ 1. Women are just as able as men to be in positions of command in the military.

_____ 2. There are currently many more women in the U.S. military than ever before.

_____ 3. It's difficult for most women to make the adjustment from military life to civilian life.

_____ 4. Military men treat military women as equals when they are serving in the military but not when they become civilians.

_____ 5. U.S. military women have the same financial benefits as men.

_____ **6.** Women serve in the military in various countries.

_____ **7.** The fact that so many women in the world are serving in the military these days shows that there are no more equality problems for women in those places.

_____ **8.** Many U.S. soldiers get a lot of letters from people they don't know.

2 _With a partner, choose one fact and one opinion from the list, and discuss ways in which you might support each one._

3 _Look back at the ideas you underlined in Prewriting Exercise 3 on page 67. Also look at the lists you made for Exercise 1A in Unit 8 of the Student Book. Make a new list of reasons to support your opinions. Include established facts to support the reasons._

WRITING THE FIRST DRAFT

Using your focused freewriting and your lists, write the first draft of your essay. You may want to include the following in your first draft:

- **First paragraph:** An introduction with a thesis statement stating your opinion. This paragraph includes either a statement listing the actual reasons you are going to use to support your opinion or a statement of your intention to support your opinion with reasons.

- **Body:** Individual paragraphs present the reasons for your opinion. Remember to use established facts and examples to support your reasons and to prove your point.

- **Last paragraph:** A concluding paragraph restates your opinion in a new way and does one or more of the following: shows how the main ideas in the body support your opinion, re-emphasizes the importance of the topic, suggests a new way to look at the topic, suggests a solution to a problem posed in your paper, and/or poses a question.

Don't worry too much about grammar while you write; just concentrate on making your ideas clear.

PEER REVIEW

When you finish your first draft, exchange papers with a partner. Read your partner's first draft. While you are reading, do the following:

- Put a check at the end of the introduction if you are in agreement with the writer's opinion as stated in the thesis statement. Put an X if you are not.

- Put a check next to the paragraph that you think best proves the author's main point.

- Underline five sentences that you think are particularly well written.

Reread your partner's paper, and do the following:

- If you didn't agree with the writer's main point before reading the first draft, do you agree now? Why or why not? If you did agree before reading the paper, do you think the writer's arguments were sufficiently effective to have convinced a doubting reader?

- Are there any points that you think are weaker than others? Make notes on how the writer could strengthen them.

- Are there any unsupported opinions or generalizations as opposed to opinions supported by verifiable facts?

- Are there any reasons that you do not understand or need more information about?

With your partner, discuss your reactions to each other's drafts. Make a note of any parts you need to revise.

3 Revising

A SUPPORTING YOUR REASONS WITH EXAMPLES

Supporting your reasons with examples is a convincing way to prove your point. Examples can be from your own personal experience, from what you know about someone else's personal experience, or from something you read. Examples can be particularly effective because they are often more memorable than facts; however, it is necessary to make sure that your examples directly support your point.

1 *Work in small groups. Discuss "Asmara Journal: In Peace, Women Warriors Rank Low," Reading Two in the Student Book. What were some of the examples presented?*

2 *The main idea of the article is that many Eritrean women feel that they were treated more as equals to men during the war than they are in peacetime. Look at the examples used to support this point. Scan the article for these examples, and write the specific point illustrated. Two are done for you.*

Example	Point Illustrated
1. Nuria Mohammed Saleh	*can find only menial work*
2. Women soldiers who intermarried	_____
3. Civilian women who worked in male-dominated professions	*after war could not keep jobs (implied)*
4. Aster Haile	_____
5. Ghenet Berhe	_____

3 *In pairs or small groups, discuss which examples you think are the most effective. Give reasons for your choices.*

4 *Reread this paragraph from Letter 1 in Reading One of the Student Book. With a partner, discuss what Thyra worries about. What example does she use to validate her worry?*

I am a First Lieutenant serving with coalition forces in the Middle East. Most of all I am afraid my husband will find out that I am within range of Iraq's Scud missiles. I don't want him to worry about me. Of course, I worry about chemical attacks. You move as fast as you can but if you get the shakes during a red alert, you can't put on your GCE [ground crew ensemble]. You can't let the fear get to you.

Note that when using examples, you can simply state your example, as Thyra Bishop did in her letter and James McKinley did in his article on Eritrean women. Alternatively, you can introduce your example with transition markers such as:

For example, . . .   As an example, . . .

A good example of this would be . . .   For instance, . . .

5 *Look at your first draft. Find places to add examples to support your reasons.*

B INCORPORATING DIRECT AND INDIRECT SPEECH

 Complete Unit 8, Section 4A, in the Student Book before you begin this section.

When using examples of people's words, you have the choice of using a direct quote or indirect speech. A direct quote can sometimes make a stronger impression and be more effective than indirect speech.

1 *Scan Reading Two in Unit 8 of the Student Book for all the uses of indirect and direct speech. Keep a tally of the number of examples of each one.*

2 *Reread the quote from the end of Reading Two.*

> But when she was asked if she missed her life in the rebel army, she smiled and said, "Of course." "We had equality," she said. "We had common goals and common ends."

With a partner, discuss why you think the author decided to quote Ghenet Berhe's exact words instead of reporting them as he had for the others. What effect is created?

3 *Choose two of the examples of indirect speech from Reading Two, and change them to direct speech, using your own words. Compare your quotations with those of another student. Do you think they are effective? What main points do you think they might be used to support?*

4 *Look at your first draft, and find places to include direct and indirect speech.*

WRITING THE SECOND DRAFT

Use the feedback you received from the peer review, your own notes, and comments from your teacher to help you revise your first draft. As you are writing, ask yourself these questions:

* Does the introduction clearly state an opinion? How I am going to support it?

* Is the essay written for a reader who might not agree with me?

* Does the essay present and explain reasons that convincingly prove the point of view?

- Are examples used to illustrate the reasons?

- Is there an effective conclusion that restates my opinion in a new way and offers something additional for the reader to think about?

- Are both direct and indirect speech incorporated?

4 Editing

PUNCTUATING DIRECT QUOTES

 Complete Unit 8, Section 4A, in the Student Book before you begin this section.

1 *Read the examples of direct quotes.*

Sentences

- But when she was asked if she missed her life in the rebel army, she smiled and said, "Of course." "We had equality," she said.

- Carla and Jillian tell us that they learned some important lessons while in the military. Carla explained, "I've learned to respect others, to survive in whatever conditions arise."

- "You do things here that you would never before dream of doing. You learn not to take things for granted," Jillian tells us.

- "Why must I sweep floors for a dollar a day?" Nuria Mohammed Saleh asked. "When I was in the army, I did the same jobs as the men, even risking my life!"

- Thyra wonders, "What will happen if I can't move fast enough in a red alert?"

Read the following six guidelines for punctuating direct quotes. Circle the correct word in parentheses.

Punctuation Guidelines

1. Put a comma (after / between) the sentence introducing the quote and the quote itself.

2. Use a (capital / small) letter to start the quote whether or not it starts the sentence.

3. If the quote is a sentence but doesn't end the sentence, put a comma (before / after) the final quotation mark and a period (following / before) the final word of the sentence.

4. If the quote is a question or an exclamation at the end of the sentence or is in the middle of the sentence, put the question mark or exclamation mark (before / after) the final quotation mark.

5. The remainder of a sentence following a quote begins with a (small / capital) letter.

6. When a new speaker begins speaking, (continue the old / start a new) paragraph.

2 *Look at your second draft. Have you used any direct speech? If so, check that you punctuated it correctly. If not, can you find any places to add direct speech?*

PREPARING THE FINAL DRAFT

Carefully edit your second draft for grammatical and mechanical errors. Use the Final Draft Checklist to help you. Finally, neatly write or type your essay.

FINAL DRAFT CHECKLIST

❏ Does the essay have an effective persuasive introduction, three or more body paragraphs, and a convincing conclusion?

❏ Does each paragraph focus on one reason or a set of related reasons to support the point of view?

❏ Are examples used to illustrate the points?

❏ Is the essay edited for correct use and punctuation of direct and indirect speech?

UNIT 9

The Cellist of Sarajevo

OVERVIEW

Theme:	The arts
Prewriting:	Questioning yourself
Organizing:	Starting narratives
Revising:	Using descriptive language
	Using the passive voice
Editing:	Using parallel structure

Assignment

In Unit 9 of *NorthStar: Reading and Writing, Advanced,* Second Edition, you read about the effect of music on two artists. Think of a work of art such as a painting, a photograph, a piece of music, a play, a dance performance, a poem, a novel, a film, or a concert that has had a strong effect on you. The assignment for this unit is to write a narrative essay telling the story of your experience with this piece of art. You will describe that time in your life, explain why the experience is so important to you, and talk about your emotional and intellectual reactions.

1 Prewriting

QUESTIONING YOURSELF

 Complete Unit 9, Sections 1–3, in the Student Book before you begin this section.

Questioning yourself as a prewriting technique is particularly appropriate for narrative writing. By questioning yourself, you are exploring your thoughts on the topic.

1 *Think about the assignment for this unit. Narrow the topic by asking yourself the following questions:*

- How does this topic relate to me?

- What relevant experiences have I had?

In pairs or small groups, discuss your answers. On your own, make a list of the various ideas that result from the discussion.

2 *From your list, further narrow your topic. Write your topic on a clean piece of paper. Then read each of the following questions, and make notes on your thoughts. Share your answers with a partner.*

1. What happened?

2. When, where, and why did it happen?

3. Who did it happen to or with?

4. How did you or the person it happened to feel about it?

5. What was important about the experience?

6. What changes has it made in your or anyone else's life?

7. What details can you or the person it happened to remember about it?

8. Why do you or the person it happened to remember it so vividly?

9. What senses were involved in the experience—that is, taste, sight, smell, hearing, or touch?

3 *Freewrite about your topic.*

2 Organizing

STARTING NARRATIVES

The first paragraph of a narrative essay should do one of two things:

- start the story

- set the scene for the story

Both ways of starting a narrative are effective ways to begin. The story you want to tell should drive your choice of how you start your narrative. Sometimes the story itself will be enough to give the reader sufficient background to understand what is happening. However, at other times you will need to set the scene for the reader so that you can influence the way the reader understands the characters and events of the story.

When the first paragraph starts the story, generally the next paragraph follows chronologically, or in order of time (see Unit 1). Note, however, that this doesn't mean that the plot has to be told from the first thing that happened to the last, although often that is the easiest way. When the first paragraph sets the scene for the story, the next paragraph is generally where the story starts chronologically.

1 *Work with a partner. Look at the first paragraph of both "The Cellist of Sarajevo" and "The Soloist," Readings One and Two in Unit 9 of the Student Book. Discuss whether the first paragraph begins the story or sets the scene. Then answer the following questions.*

1. What does the first paragraph of "The Cellist of Sarajevo" explain? Why do you think the author feels this is necessary for the reader to know at this time? How does it help the reader to understand the rest of the narrative?

2. What does the first paragraph of "The Soloist" tell you about? How do you feel when you read the first sentences? When do you discover the significance of the actions explained in the first paragraph?

3. Which of the two first paragraphs drew you in faster?

4. Which of the two first paragraphs helped you to understand earlier the significance of the incident related?

2 *Imagine that the first paragraph of "The Soloist" is the first paragraph of the body. Write an introductory first paragraph that sets the scene for the story to follow. Share your paragraph in a small group. Discuss whether you think "The Soloist" is better with or without your introductory paragraphs. Give reasons.*

3 *Reread "The Cellist of Sarajevo" without the introductory first paragraph. In your groups, discuss the differences in the way the reader would understand the story. Say which way you think is better. Give reasons.*

4 *Look back at your notes from the Prewriting exercises on page 76. What do you want the purpose of your first paragraph to be? Write the first paragraph of your essay.*

5 *Look back at your notes, and think about how you want to organize the body of your essay. Make an outline of the events and when they happened.*

WRITING THE FIRST DRAFT

Use your notes from the Prewriting section, your freewriting, and the paragraph and outline you wrote in the Organizing section to write the first draft of your essay. You may want to include the following in your first draft:

- **First paragraph:** This begins the story or sets the scene.

- **Body:** Individual paragraphs tell the rest of the story. Remember to use appropriate time words and phrases to clearly state the time relationships between events.

- **Last Paragraph:** A concluding paragraph brings your narrative to a close and re-emphasizes the significance of the experience in your life.

Don't worry too much about grammar while you write; just concentrate on making your ideas clear.

PEER REVIEW

When you finish your first draft, exchange papers with a partner. Read your partner's first draft. While you are reading, do the following:

- Put a check beside the paragraph that you think is the most important part of the story.

- Underline five sentences that you think are particularly well written.

Reread your partner's paper, and do the following:

- Does the first paragraph start the story or set the scene? If it starts the story, note whether you think a scene-setting paragraph is necessary.

- Note whether the story is easy to follow chronologically.

- Decide if there are any points in the story that are confusing or that you would like to know more about.

- Note whether you think the ending is a good one.

- Is the role of art in the story sufficiently clear and important?

With your partner, discuss your reactions to each other's drafts. Make a note of any parts you need to revise.

3 Revising

A   USING DESCRIPTIVE LANGUAGE

 Complete Unit 9, Section 4B, in the Student Book before you begin this section.

Using descriptive language in your writing helps the reader to visualize the story as if he or she were watching a movie or TV show, or even as if the reader were in the story. The reader will feel the mood and the feelings of the characters and hear the sounds and see the sights the characters hear and see. Adding adjectives, adjective phrases and clauses, adverbs, and descriptive verbs can help your readers to:

- visualize the physical setting and characters
- feel the characters' emotions and feelings
- hear the sounds the characters heard
- feel the mood of the atmosphere

1 *Read the following two paragraphs. Note the differences in descriptive language between the two paragraphs. Then underline the descriptive techniques used in the second paragraph.*

Paragraph 1

After improvising for a while, I started playing a song. Freed of the task of finding the right phrasing, the right intonation, the right bowing, I heard the music through my skin. For the first time I didn't think about how it would sound to anyone else, and I started to hear again. I played the notes slowly at first, then more quickly. After a while I looked up and saw the cat sitting in front of me. I had an audience again. (Adapted from *The Soloist*)

Paragraph 2

After improvising for a while, I started playing the D minor Bach suite, still in the darkness. Strangely freed of the task of finding the right phrasing, the right intonation, the right bowing, I heard the music through my skin. For the first time I didn't think about how it would sound to anyone else, and slowly, joyfully, gratefully, I started to hear again. The notes sang out, first like a trickle, then like a fountain of cool water bubbling up from a hole in the middle of a desert. After an hour or so I looked up, and in the darkness saw the outline of the cat sitting on the floor in front of me, cleaning her paws and purring loudly. I had an audience again, humble as it was. (From *The Soloist*)

2 *Work in pairs, and discuss the descriptive techniques used in the second paragraph. Do these techniques create any of the effects listed on page 79? Which ones?*

3 *With your partner, scan "The Cellist of Sarajevo" in the Student Book for at least two examples of each type of descriptive writing.*

4 *Look at your first draft. Did you use details to help the reader visualize the physical setting and characters, feel the characters' emotions and feelings, hear the sounds or smell the smells, and feel the mood of the atmosphere? Find places to add these types of details to your story.*

B ■ USING THE PASSIVE VOICE

 Complete Unit 9, Section 4A, in the Student Book before you begin this section.

The passive voice is used mainly for reporting facts, ideas, and events when:

- the agent is unknown

  The song was written sometime in the eighteenth century.

- the agent is unimportant in that instance

  The bakery was destroyed.

- the writer wants the reader to focus on the fact, idea, or event rather than the agent

  Their lives were forever enriched.

- the writer wants to distance himself or herself from the fact, idea, or event

  It has often been said that time heals all wounds, but it didn't in this case.

In all other cases, the active voice is used.

Note in the examples that the subjects in the passive voice structures are always the recipients of actions. They are never the "doers" of actions. In other words, they are passive as opposed to active.

1 *Look at the following sentences from "The Cellist of Sarajevo." With a partner, discuss which of the reasons listed above would explain why the author chose to use the passive voice.*

1. As a pianist, I was invited to perform with cellist Eugene Friesen at the International Cello Festival in Manchester, England.

2. Though the shellings went on, he was never hurt.

3. . . . . an English composer, David Wilde, was so moved that he, too, decided to make music.

4. We were all stripped down to our starkest, deepest humanity at encountering this man who shook his cello in the face of bombs, death and ruin, defying them all.

5. Then I was struck by the profound similarities.

2 *Only one sentence in Exercise 1 above explicitly identifies an agent. Which sentence is it? What is the agent?*

3 *With your partner, put the sentences in Exercise 1 above in the active voice. Refer to "The Cellist of Sarajevo" to establish who or what the agent should be. Discuss the differences in meaning and effect.*

4 *Look at your first draft. Did you use the passive voice, and if so, did you use it appropriately and correctly? To check for appropriateness, try changing your passive sentences to active sentences. Are there any differences in meaning, effect, or focus? If you don't have any sentences in the passive voice, look for a place to put one; alternatively, change one active sentence to a passive sentence.*

WRITING THE SECOND DRAFT

Use the feedback you received from the peer review, your own notes, and comments from your teacher to help you revise your first draft. As you are writing, ask yourself these questions:

- Does the introduction effectively start the story or set the scene in an interesting and engaging way?

- Is the role of art in the story clear?

- Does the conclusion bring the story to an end?

- Are descriptive details used to involve the reader?

- Are there any sentences in the passive voice?

4 Editing

USING PARALLEL STRUCTURE

 Complete Unit 9, Section 4B, in the Student Book before you begin this section.

Using parallel structure helps you to involve your reader in your story by the rhythmic patterns it creates. It can also create specific moods such as calm, excitement, or even suspense.

- Parallel structure can be achieved by repeating words or phrases within a sentence:

Strangely freed of the task of finding the right phrasing, the right intonation, the right bowing, I heard the music through my skin.

- Parallel structure can also be achieved through repeated sentence types:

Our piece was completed but no one clapped. He put down his violin, closed his music book, and slowly got up from his chair. I put down my cello, closed my music book, and got up from my chair. We faced the audience and bowed together. Together, the audience stood up and applauded.

All the repeated structures must be grammatically similar. Therefore, if the structure you are repeating is a noun, the repeated structures must all be nouns; if it is a prepositional phrase, the repeated phrase or phrases must be prepositional phrases.

1 *Complete the sentences with parallel structures.*

1. This play was written, directed, and _____ by the children of the Williston Community Home.

2. He unveiled the painting. We gasped. How could he have known? Who could have told him? _____

3. The sculptor appeared neither pleased by nor _____ of his work.

4. The movie director played with our emotions, bombarded us with violent images, and _____.

2 *Look at your second draft. Have you used any parallel structures? If so, check for accuracy. If not, find three places to make the necessary alterations to include parallel structures.*

PREPARING THE FINAL DRAFT

Carefully edit your second draft for grammatical and mechanical errors. Use the Final Draft Checklist to help you. Finally, neatly write or type your essay.

FINAL DRAFT CHECKLIST

❏ Does the essay have an effective and engaging beginning?

❏ Does each paragraph focus on one or a series of connected events?

❏ Are descriptive details used to "illustrate" the plot?

❏ Is the essay unified and coherent?

❏ Does the story come to a satisfying end?

❏ Does the conclusion offer the reader something to reflect on concerning the story?

❏ Is the essay edited for passive and active voice and use of parallelism?

UNIT **10**

The Right to Read

OVERVIEW

Theme:	First Amendment issues
Prewriting:	Choosing a technique
Organizing:	Including counterarguments and refutations
Revising:	Writing persuasive introductions
	Using tenses correctly
Editing:	Proofreading

Assignment

In Unit 10 of *NorthStar: Reading and Writing, Advanced,* Second Edition, you read about freedom of speech and censorship. There are censorship laws in the United States about how old a child or teen needs to be to view sex and/or violence in movies without parental consent. Songs with profane lyrics are often censored on the radio. Profane language, explicit sex, and nudity are also censored from many programs and films shown on TV. What is your opinion of restricting the age of moviegoers or of censoring language from music on the radio or in films and programs on TV? The assignment for this unit is to write an argumentative essay either for or against censorship in the media and the arts.

1 Prewriting

CHOOSING A TECHNIQUE

 Complete Unit 10, Sections 1–3, in the Student Book before you begin this section.

There are various prewriting techniques for generating ideas. Although some types of techniques lend themselves better to specific writing genres—for example, flowcharts for cause-and-effect essays and Venn diagrams for comparison and contrast essays—all the others can be used with any writing genre.

If there is one technique with which you are most comfortable, that is probably the technique that will work best for you. Many writers find, however, that a combination of techniques works well for them. Remember that freewriting is a useful tool either by itself or as a means to consolidate your ideas in preparation for or follow-up to other prewriting techniques.

1 *Work in pairs or small groups. Review the following list of prewriting techniques, and discuss what is involved in each one.*

Freewriting (Unit 1)

Critical listing (Unit 2)

Flowchart (Units 3 and 4)

Venn diagram (Unit 5)

Looped freewriting (Unit 6)

Clustering (Unit 7)

Focused freewriting (Unit 8)

Questioning yourself (Unit 9)

2 *To narrow your specific topic for this writing assignment, use the two general questions from the questioning yourself technique (see Unit 9) and/or freewrite about the writing assignment. Note that a good argumentative topic has at least two sides to the argument—sides both for and against your position. In addition, the reasons you use to argue your position must be supported by facts rather than opinions.*

3 *Think about the assignment for this unit. Write one or two possible topics. Then work with a partner and discuss your topic(s). Make notes, and then choose your own topic. Finally, use one or two of the prewriting techniques listed to generate ideas for your topic.*

2 Organizing

INCLUDING COUNTERARGUMENTS AND REFUTATIONS

 Complete Unit 10, Section 4B, in the Student Book before you begin this section.

An effective argumentative essay:

* argues the writer's position by stating and supporting the writer's own opinions

* convincingly refutes opposing points of view, or counterarguments, while conceding valid opposing points of view

These two strategies working together to make your essay persuasive can change your readers' opinions about your topic.

An argumentative essay can be organized in one of three ways:

1. Make your own arguments, followed by the counterarguments and refutations.

2. Alternate between your own arguments and the relevant counterarguments and refutations.

3. Discuss the counterarguments and refutations, then follow with your own arguments.

Which organizational pattern you choose depends on which you think is more persuasive—your own arguments or the refutations to the counterarguments. Remember, however, that counterarguments are relevant only if they directly counter one of your main points.

1 *Skim "Book Banning Must Be Stopped," Reading One in Unit 10 of the Student Book. Write **P** next to a paragraph that presents one of Marcia Cohen's positions and **CR** next to a paragraph that presents a counterargument and refutation. Then work with a partner, and discuss which of the three organizational styles listed was used by Marcia Cohen to argue her position on book banning.*

2 *With your partner, discuss the effectiveness of Marcia Cohen's refutations. Remember that refutations must address each part of a counterargument. If a refutation addresses only part of the counterargument, it is not an effective refutation. Does Cohen refute each of the counterarguments persuasively?*

Notice the difference in strength between saying that something is *considered* dangerous as opposed to saying that something *is* dangerous. Likewise, notice the difference in strength between "The censors may mean well" and "The censors mean well." Weak modals and verbs of perception are used to state counterarguments.

3 *Read the following excerpts of counterarguments from Reading One, and underline the words and phrases that weaken the position of the counterargument. The first one is done for you.*

1. ". . . <u>considered</u> 'dangerous' because . . ."

2. "Often under the guise of upholding community values . . ."

3. "Apparently they believe that . . ."

4. "The censors may mean well; however, . . ."

5. "In Oregon, environmentalists wanted to remove a social studies book because they believed it contained . . ."

6. "The group argued that . . ."

7. ". . . a doctrine that they said . . ."

4 *Reread the letter in Unit 10 of the Student Book, pages 236–237. Elizabeth Jones's arguments are based on her own opinions. Her letter does not address relevant counterarguments. With your partner, make a list of three counterarguments Jones could have added to her letter to make it more persuasive. Then rewrite three of Jones's paragraphs to include the new counterarguments, making her arguments into refutations or adding new refutations. Remember to use weak modals to state the counterarguments.*

5 *Look back at your prewriting, and on another piece of paper make a two-column table like the one below.*

1. Write your topic at the top.

2. Make a list of your arguments to support your position.

3. Make a list of the counterarguments.

4. Make a list of the corresponding refutations when they are different from your arguments.

TOPIC	
Supporting Arguments	Counterarguments and Refutations

6 *Look back at your prewriting, your notes, and the table you made, and think about how you will organize your essay. Make an outline ordering your arguments, counterarguments, and refutations.*

WRITING THE FIRST DRAFT

Use your prewriting notes and/or freewriting, your table from Organizing Exercise 5, and your outline to write the first draft of your essay. You may want to include the following in your first draft:

- **First paragraph:** The introduction states the issue and your position.

- **Body:** Individual paragraphs state your persuasive main points with ample support, your counterarguments and refutations, and at least one concession.

- **Last paragraph:** A concluding paragraph restates your argument in a new way and re-emphasizes the importance of your topic or your position. It could also suggest what might happen if your position isn't acted on or taken into account.

Don't worry too much about grammar while you write; just concentrate on making your ideas clear.

PEER REVIEW

When you finish your first draft, exchange papers with a partner. Read your partner's first draft. While you are reading, do the following:

- Put a check beside the issue or problem, and underline the writer's position on it.

- Put a check beside the paragraph that you think is the strongest support for the argument.

- Number all the counterarguments and the corresponding refutations.

Reread your partner's paper, and do the following:

- Note whether you think all the writer's main points are logical arguments. Note any you think are weak and why.

- Decide if you think the refutations are effective against the counterarguments.

- Note whether there are any concessions. If there aren't any, suggest where one might be added.

- Point out any paragraphs that are confusing to you or that you would like to know more about.

With your partner, discuss your reactions to each other's drafts. Make a note of any parts you need to revise.

3 Revising

A WRITING PERSUASIVE INTRODUCTIONS

 Complete Unit 10, Section 4B, in the Student Book before you begin this section.

As in all introductions, the argumentative essay introduction should contain these three parts:

1. an interesting and engaging opener

2. background information

3. a thesis statement

Openers

In the argumentative essay, the introduction has to be interesting enough to convince skeptical readers to read the essay. It must immediately involve the reader. Ways to do this include making a provocative statement, using a quotation, or asking a question of the reader.

1 *How does Cohen involve the reader in her introduction of "Book Banning Must Be Stopped," Reading One in the Student Book?*

2 *Put a check (✓) beside openers you think immediately involve the reader and an **X** beside the ones that don't.*

_____ **1.** As soon as I entered the classroom, everyone stopped talking, turned to look at me, and started laughing.

_____ **2.** My children went to a bad movie last week.

_____ **3.** The smell of burning paper filled the air, and the sound of jubilant whooping resounded throughout the woods.

_____ **4.** I'm writing to say that people should be able to see any movie they want.

_____ **5.** How would you feel if you were extremely mature for your age, and hung out mainly with older teens, but couldn't go with your friends just because of a movie rating?

3 *Reread your introduction. Make sure your introduction has a good, interesting, and engaging opener. If it doesn't, write one now.*

Background Information and Thesis Statement

The background information in an argumentative essay introduction presents the issue and leads to the thesis statement. The thesis statement clearly states the author's position and can also make a strong suggestion about the issue. Most commonly this is done through the use of modals such as *should (not), must (not), would be better if . . . , would like you to . . .*

4 *Read the following paragraph. Underline the background information, and put parentheses around the thesis statement. Then compare with a partner.*

As soon as I entered the classroom, everyone stopped talking, turned to look at me, and started laughing. Mr. Ridell looked up from his record book and frowned. I knew today was not going to be easy, but I had no regrets. This morning, I had chosen to wear a T-shirt with a picture of a well-respected painting on it. OK, so neither the man nor the woman in the picture was wearing any clothes, but the original painting hangs in the Louvre, which makes it pretty respectable in the eyes of the world. The week before, the school board had instituted a new dress code, and the picture on my T-shirt clearly violated the new dress code. But this T-shirt reflects me and who I am, especially my artistic side. Students shouldn't be prevented from wearing clothes to school that express their inner selves just because some people might be offended.

5 *Look back at the book summaries in Reading Two of Unit 10 in the Student Book. Imagine that you want to write an argumentative essay either supporting or arguing against the censoring of any or all of these books. Write an introduction for this essay. Discuss your introduction with a partner.*

6 *Look at your first draft, and rewrite your introduction. Check that the body of your essay is a logical extension of your introduction. Make sure your introduction includes an engaging opener, useful background information, and a strong, persuasive thesis statement that clearly states your position.*

B   USING TENSES CORRECTLY

 Complete Unit 10, Section 4A, in the Student Book before you begin this section.

1 *Read the following paragraph. The tenses are not all used consistently. Underline the inconsistencies, and correct them. Then compare your answers with a partner. Give reasons for your changes.*

Most of the teachers and parents support the new dress code about T-shirts because they claimed that wearing T-shirts with certain designs on them causes distractions for both the teachers and students. But the truth was that designs on T-shirts don't distract students. The students won't get distracted because they saw these types of T-shirts all the time outside of school. Last week I had been at the mall, and there have been kids there in all sorts of T-shirts, even ones I would never wear. No one seems to be paying any attention but the adults. It has always been the same thing at school. Before the dress code, when a kid wore something outlandish, the only thing that happens was another kid might say "Cool shirt!" or something like that. But now, since the new code goes into effect, everyone stops to stare and got very distracted waiting to see what happened.

2 *Look at your first draft. Check for consistency in your use of tenses. If there are any verbs you are unsure about, ask another student or your teacher.*

WRITING THE SECOND DRAFT

Use the feedback you received from the peer review, your own notes, and comments from your teacher to help you revise your first draft. As you are writing, ask yourself these questions:

- Does the introduction effectively engage the reader, explain the issue, and state a position?

- Do all the paragraphs directly support this position with facts and examples?

- Are the most common counterarguments taken into account, and are they refuted well?

- Have any concessions to valid counterarguments been made and been shown not to weaken the position?

- Does the conclusion follow logically from the arguments? Does it offer any suggestions for the future, if relevant?

- Is the essay edited for correct use and form of all verb tenses?

4 Editing

PROOFREADING

When you proofread, you read for correctness as opposed to content. You proofread after you have decided that you are satisfied with the content of your essay. Proofreading involves reading each individual word and phrase carefully, stopping frequently to ask yourself questions.

Proofread your second draft. You may find these three proofreading techniques useful.

1. Read each sentence out loud. Then reread, and make your eyes stop at each word, phrase, and sentence while you consider it for accuracy.

2. Correct any errors you can.

3. Proofread again for words, phrases, sentences, and/or punctuation marks you are unsure of. Underline or circle them.

PREPARING THE FINAL DRAFT

Carefully edit your second draft for grammatical and mechanical errors. Use the Final Draft Checklist to help you. Finally, neatly write or type your essay.

FINAL DRAFT CHECKLIST

- ❏ Does the essay have an effective and engaging opener? Does the introduction include background information and a strongly-worded thesis statement?

- ❏ Does each paragraph focus on one or a set of related supporting arguments?

- ❏ Is each argument well supported with facts and examples?

- ❏ Does each reason or set of reasons logically argue your position as stated in the thesis statement?

- ❏ Is the essay unified and coherent?

- ❏ Is the essay edited for verb tenses?

- ❏ Have you proofread your essay?

Answer Key

Note: For exercises where no answers are given, answers will vary.

UNIT 1

2 Organizing (pages 3–4)

1
- The chronology is linear: from past to present.
- The essay begins with an introduction about the topic—Mickey Mantle's addiction—and how he believes that his addiction was a result of heredity, since his mother's brothers were all addicts.
- The body of the essay tells about Mickey's father, his relationship with his father, how Mickey's addiction began, and what he did about it.
- The conclusion summarizes his life up until then and how he hopes it will be in the future.

2
- The first paragraph describes the beginning of the daughter's television addiction.
- The second paragraph describes what caused the daughter to develop an addiction.
- Answers will vary.

3 When she was 14 years old . . . ; After school . . . ; . . . and then . . . ; In the beginning . . . ; . . . but after a few months . . . ; . . . when she was 13 years old and in junior high school; That year . . . ; First . . . ; . . . when we moved to a new town; . . . a few weeks after school began . . . ; Within only a few weeks . . .

3 Revising (pages 6–8)

A

1 *Possible answers:* depressed, emotional, sad, has difficulty talking about family, aware of faults, irresponsible, feels guilt

2 *Possible answers:* lonely, insecure, difficulties making friends, shy

B

1 1. If he had had my dad / he could have been a major league baseball player.

   Reality (answers will vary): My son didn't have my dad, so he didn't learn how to be a great athlete.

   2. I would have been better off / if I could have told him that a long time ago.

   Reality (answers will vary): I wasn't better off because I didn't tell my father how I felt a long time ago.

4 Editing (page 8)

1 *Correct forms:* manageable; determined; tough; surviving; avoid; prioritized; denied

UNIT 2

2 Organizing (pages 12–13)

1 1. B2 2. C 3. I 4. B1

2 1. We need to once again explore utopian ideas—through science fiction novels or dystopian films—as a first step toward creating a better future.

2. The thesis is stated at the end of the introduction.

3. The body paragraphs support the thesis by giving examples of how utopian and dystopian visions can move us toward a better future. In the first body paragraph, the author explores how writers use science fiction to imaginitively create new utopian societies. In the second body paragraph, the author explores dystopian visions in movies and explains that they are examples of the terrible things that could happen if we do not change.

4. Ultimately, both dystopian visions and imagined utopias are important ways to analyze our present world and work toward a better future.

3 Revising (pages 14–17)

A

1 4 and 5

2 1. T: Why utopias are sought but never become reality

   TS: Because of the competitive and destructive aspects of human nature, utopias will always be an impossible dream.

2. To provide some interesting historical background and context

3. They further explain the topic.

4. d, e, f

5. The next paragraphs will explore and give examples of specific competitive and destructive aspects of human nature.

B

1

1. What ~~have utopians~~ *utopians have* never realized is that human nature will never allow a group to live peacefully and equitably.

2. Why *people* choose to establish utopian communities is perfectly understandable.

3. It isn't always possible to know ~~why~~ *what* the best solution to these problems is.

4. I'm not persuaded by your argument *about* how ~~does~~ human nature prevents people from creating a better society.

5. ~~Our~~ *That our* society is unjust ~~that~~ was agreed upon by everyone.

4 Editing (page 17)

1 *Possible answers:*

1. One of the oldest utopian ideals is communism. *Plato's Republic* was communist, as was More's and that of Edward Bellamy. The Soviet Union never fully achieved a communist society because it expected the impossible—that people be less selfish than they are.

2. Utopians often exclude bad or weak types of people. In *Plato's Republic,* men and women were paired off to create smarter, stronger children. The Nazis also wanted to purify and improve the race. If that is utopia, my vote would be to make do with the world we've got.

UNIT 3

2 Organizing (pages 21–23)

1 The main idea is that some successful people are not happy despite their successes. The two well-known people the author uses as examples are Judy Garland and Marilyn Monroe.

2 1. j   2. c   3. d, e

3 1. a   2. hope   3. b   4. c
5. Three sentences—d, e, f

3 Revising (pages 24–26)

B

1 1. which   2. that/which   3. whom   4. who
5. whose; which

4 Editing (pages 26–28)

1 1. S   2. P   3. S   4. P   5. P   6. S
7. S   8. S   9. S

2 1. is   2. were   3. are/were   4. was

UNIT 4

2 Organizing (pages 31–32)

1 1. effects   2. causal chain

3 Revising (pages 33–36)

A

1 *Unrelated details:* Large recalls of contaminated meat from non-organic sources; Most popular foods in the United States; Good publicity on other food trends.

2 *Possible answer:* Carson's book, *Silent Spring,* laid the foundation for today's environmental protection movement.

3 One of the landmark books of the twentieth century, *Silent Spring* still speaks to us today, many years after its publication.

B

1 *Introduce a cause:* because; since
Introduce an effect: so; therefore; consequently; thus

2 *Introduce a cause:* from, due to
Introduce an effect: was caused by; as a consequence of; resulting in; as a consequence; a direct result of

1. C; from
2. C; As a direct result of
3. C; was caused by
4. E; resulting in
5. C; due to
6. E; as a consequence
7. C; due to

4 Editing (page 37)

1 1. S   2. C   3. CC   4. CS   5. CS

UNIT 5

1 Prewriting (pages 39–41)

1 Elizabeth is the left side and Eva is the right.

2 1

2 Organizing (pages 41–43)

4 *Suggested answers:*
1. B   2. PBP   3. PBP   4. B

3 Revising (pages 43–46)

A

1 *Possible answers:*

1. subtle differences in North American and Asian business practices; obvious differences in North American and Asian business practices; reasons for and results of cross-cultural training

2. similarities between food sources for the Xantax and the Qabal; the differences between their traditional diets; a comparison of the old-age diseases in both groups

3. differences between American and Samoan teenagers' relationships with their parents; differences in American and Samoan parents' methods of discipline; differences in American and Samoan parents' expectations for help; differences in the amount of time American and Samoan parents spend with their children; how these differences affect relationships

2 *Possible answers:*

"Lost in Translation": It is difficult to be true to what your immigrant parents expect of you and fit into your new society.

"The Struggle to Be an All-American Girl": As an American born child of immigrants, it is very hard to be American without losing your ties to your parents' culture.

B

1 *Adverbials used to compare and contrast between clauses:* Like Eva . . . ; In the same way that Eva . . . ; Just as Eva is angered . . . ; Unlike Eva . . . ; Whereas Eva embraces . . . ; While Eva wants . . . ; In contrast to Elizabeth . . . ; Whereas Eva sees herself . . . ; . . . while Elizabeth is only . . . ; whereas Eva herself . . .

Words and phrases used to compare and contrast within clauses: . . . both Eva Hoffman and Elizabeth Wong . . . ; . . . although Eva and Elizabeth may have certain . . . ; Elizabeth also hates it . . . ; Eva and Elizabeth are both unhappy . . . ; Both Eva and Elizabeth are more outwardly . . . ; Although Eva and Elizabeth share . . . ; . . . children like Eva . . . ; . . . children like Elizabeth . . .

4 Editing (page 46)

1 simple

UNIT 6

3 Revising (pages 52–54)

A

1 *Answers may vary.*

1. d, h 2. c, g, h 3. a, c 4. b
5. c, f 6. a, c 7. c, g 8. e

B

1

NC honesty	C/NC law	C/NC belief
C/NC principle	NC knowledge	C ritual
C/NC evil	NC generosity	NC forgiveness
NC reincarnation	C/NC prayer	NC hypocrisy
C symbol	C/NC faith	C/NC kindness
NC goodness	C/NC commitment	C/NC creation
C guideline	C tenet	C/NC acceptance
C/NC (in)tolerance	C/NC charity	C/NC tradition
C/NC death		

4 Editing (pages 54–55)

1
1. ten 5. can / cannot
2. one word 6. five
3. aren't 7. even if
4. can

UNIT 7

1 Prewriting (pages 57–59)

1 starting my own business

2 *Negative ideas:* planning/preparation; need many skills—marketing, financial; need to go to school or work at a company to get these skills; financial risks; income is not steady; high failure rate for new businesses; may lose money of friends and relatives who helped bankroll the business; may lose all own money; with success, may spend more time on administrative and legal matters; might not be interesting or useful to others; may fail; long hours; no time for family life or social life; no vacations; responsible for failures; work harder; have to meet customer demands; customer is real boss.

The rest are generally positive.

2 Organizing (pages 59–61)

1 *Reading One*

1. The audience is people who may start their own businesses.

2. The writer's purpose is to give some examples of successful young entrepreneurs, who may be role models.

3. Dineh Monajer does not want to be an entrepreneur. In paragraph 4, she mentions disadvantages such as dealing with budgets and stocks.

4. The article focuses more on the advantages of entrepreneurship.

5. Possible conclusion: Becoming an entrepreneur at a young age can be risky, but the potential advantages are so great that it is worth the risk.

6. Answers will vary, but the reading would probably support the advantages of entrepreneurship.

Reading Two

1. The article is from a business textbook.

2. The audience is probably business students or human-relations professionals from other international companies.

3. Coca-Cola's success can be explained by its human-resource management strategies, which emphasize multiculturalism.

4. The article mentions four approaches. They are all important. No disadvantages are mentioned; the article is only about the advantages of multicultural, multilingual staff.

5. Answers will vary, but the reading would probably support the advantages of working for a large multinational company.

3 Revising (pages 62–64)

A

1 "The company's human-resource management strategy helps to explain how Coke is able to achieve this feat."

2 "Coca-Cola believes that these approaches are extremely useful in helping the firm to find talent on a global basis."

3 The conclusion restates the thesis in a new way, adding a new twist or way of thinking about the topic. It also re-emphasizes the importance of the topic so that the reader feels he or she has learned something.

B

1

2. I think I have a natural ability *to* run a business.

4. I do not think I would have any difficulty in getting clients to ~~trusting~~ *trust* me and even to ~~relying~~ *rely* on me.

5. After ~~work~~ *working* for some years, I would be very interested in ~~have~~ *having* the responsibility for expanding my business.

4 Editing (page 65)

1 2. SD 3. SD 4. OI 5. SD 6. OI 7. OI

2 1. One advantage is that 2. In addition, 3. For instance, 4. most important, 5. One disadvantage is that 6. especially 7. More important

UNIT 8

2 Organizing (pages 68–69)

1 *Facts:* 2, 5, 6, and 8

3 Revising (pages 70–73)

A

2 2. families rejected their marriages; employers were reluctant to hire them for skilled jobs

4. many men resist treating her like a businesswoman

5. misses her life in the rebel army because she had equality and common goals and ends

4 Thyra worries about her husband finding out that she is within range of Iraq's Scud missiles and also about chemical attacks. Example: ". . . if you get the shakes during a red alert, you can't put on your GCE."

B

1 *Indirect speech:* 7
Direct speech: 1

2 The effect is stronger because the reader is able to see the main point through the eyes of one of the women who lived the experience.

4 Editing (pages 73–74)

1 1. between 2. capital 3. before; following 4. before 5. small 6. start a new

UNIT 9

2 Organizing (pages 76–77)

1 The first paragraph of "The Cellist of Sarajevo" sets the scene, and the first paragraph of "The Soloist" begins the story.

1. The first paragraph of "The Cellist of Sarajevo" explains the purpose of the International Cello Festival and discusses the type of people who attend. The setting helps to prepare the reader to appreciate the significance of what follows. Knowing this, the reader should be more interested in the story.

2. The first paragraph of "The Soloist" tells about why the author tried playing the cello without a shirt on and what the experience was like. The first sentences make the reader eager to find out what happens next. The reader discovers the significance of the actions mainly in the conclusion.

3. Answers will vary.

4. the first paragraph of "The Cellist of Sarajevo"

3 Revising (pages 79–81)

A

1 *Paragraph 2.* After improvising for a while, I started playing the <u>D minor Bach suite, still in the darkness</u>. <u>Strangely</u> freed of the task of finding the right phrasing, the right intonation, the right bowing, I heard the music through my skin. For the first time I didn't think about how it would sound to anyone else, and <u>slowly, joyfully, gratefully,</u> I started to hear again. <u>The notes sang out, first like a trickle, then like a fountain of cool water bubbling up from a hole in the middle of a desert</u>. After <u>an hour or so</u> I looked up, and <u>in the darkness saw the outline of</u> the cat sitting <u>on the floor</u> in front of me, <u>cleaning her paws and purring loudly</u>. I had an audience again, <u>humble as it was</u>.

2 the D minor Bach suite: Hear the sounds the characters heard; Feel the mood of the atmosphere

still in the darkness: Visualize the physical setting and characters; Feel the mood of the atmosphere

Strangely: Feel the characters' emotions and feelings

slowly, joyfully, gratefully: Feel the characters' emotions and feelings

The notes sang out, first like a trickle, then like a fountain of cool water bubbling up from a hole in the middle of a desert: Hear the sounds the characters heard; Feel the characters' emotions and feelings

an hour or so: Feel the mood of the atmosphere

in the darkness saw the outline of: Visualize the physical setting and characters

on the floor: Visualize the physical setting and characters

cleaning her paws and purring loudly: Visualize the physical setting and characters

humble as it was: Visualize the physical setting and characters; feel the characters' emotions and feelings

B

2 Sentence 5 ("profound similarities" is the agent)

3 1. The organizers of the International Cello Festival in Manchester, England, invited me to perform as a pianist with cellist Eugene Friesen.

2. Though the shellings went on, none of the bullets or bombs ever hurt him.

3. . . . Vedran Smailovic's actions so moved David Wilde, an English composer, that he, too, decided to make music.

4. Encountering this man who shook his cello in the face of bombs, death, and ruin, defying them all, stripped us all down to our starkest, deepest humanity.

5. Then the profound similarities struck me.

4 Editing (page 82)

1 *Answers will vary. Possible answers:*

1. performed
2. Why would he have done this?
3. proud
4. confused us with the contradictory ending

UNIT 10

2 Organizing (pages 86–87)

1 P: paragraphs 1, 4, 5, 8, 9, 10, 11

CR: paragraphs 2, 3, 6, 7

Marcia Cohen used organizational style 2.

3 2. under the guise of
3. Apparently; believe
4. may
5. they believed
6. argued that
7. they said

3 Revising (pages 89–92)

A

1 She uses a direct quote.

4 This morning, I had chosen to wear a T-shirt with a picture of a well-respected painting on it. OK, so neither the man nor the woman in the picture was wearing any clothes, but the original painting hangs in the Louvre, which makes it pretty respectable in the eyes of the world. The week before, the school board had instituted a new dress code, and the picture on my T-shirt clearly violated the new dress code. But this T-shirt reflects me and who I am, especially my artistic side. (Students shouldn't be prevented from wearing clothes to school that express their inner selves just because some people might be offended.)

B (page 91)

1 Most of the teachers and parents support the new dress code about T-shirts because they ~~claimed~~ *claim* that wearing T-shirts with certain designs on them causes distractions for both the teachers and students. But the truth ~~was~~ *is* that designs on T-shirts don't distract students. The students ~~won't~~ *don't* get distracted because they ~~saw~~ *see* these types of T-shirts all the time outside of school. Last week I ~~had been~~ *was* at the mall and there ~~have been~~ *were* kids there in all sorts of T-shirts, even ones that I would never wear. No one ~~seems~~ *seemed* to be paying any attention but the adults. It ~~has always been~~ *is always/has always been* the same thing at school. Before the dress code, when a kid wore something outlandish, the only thing that ~~happens~~ *happened* was another kid might say "Cool shirt!" or something like that. But now, since the new code ~~goes~~ *went* into effect, everyone stops to stare and ~~got~~ *gets* very distracted waiting to see what ~~happened~~ *will happen*.

Notes

Notes

Notes

Notes